914·29

AEROFILMS GUIDE

Offa's Dyke (South) and the River Wye Valley

OFFA'S DYKE (SOUTH) AND THE RIVER WYE VALLEY

Based on an original idea by
Richard Cox of Aerofilms

Designers Michael D. Stride and
Robert C. Wilcockson
Series Editor Rebecca King

Published by Ian Allan Ltd, Shepperton, Surrey;
and printed at their works at Coomblands in
Runnymede, England

Text © Ian Allan Ltd 1993
Photographs © Aerofilms 1993

First published 1993

ISBN 0 7110 21341

Contents

Inset: Seven Sisters Rock, near Symonds Yat
Main picture: Flanesford Priory, near Goodrich
Title page: Dinedor Camp, near Hereford

Other titles in this series:

The Cotswold Way

The South Devon Coast Path

The South Downs Way

The Thames Path

The Leeds-Liverpool Canal

Followin

Offa's Dyke Path: The path is waymarked using substantial oakwood signposts marked 'Offa's Dyke Path' or the Welsh 'Llwyber Clawdd Offa'. Other waymarking is by metal discs - bearing an acorn sym

DIRECTION
In general, the right-hand edge of the photo-map joins the left-hand edge of the map on the next spread. However, to make the direction of the route absolutely clear, arrows indicate how the maps link together.

SECTIONS OF THE PATH
Each route has been divided into sections that can be tackled in a day. These sections open with an introduction and the distance involved is given.

OBLIQUE PHOTOGRAPHS
These photographs bring a new perspective to the landscape and its buildings. All the subjects chosen can either be seen from, lie on, or are within easy reach of the path.

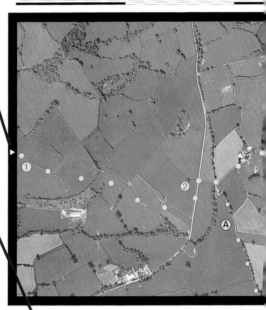

Pandy to Llantilio Crossenny

8 miles (12.8km)

The next section of the path leading south from Pandy to Llantilio Crossenny takes the walker through the quiet farming country of the Welsh Marches. On the way the rou passes two fine churches, the impressive White Castle and several country inns.

Tudor Llandilangel Court (not open)

SYMBOLS
The following symbols appear on the photo-maps for information and to help the walker get his bearings.

 Railway station

 Place of interest

Pub or hotel

P Car park

 Church

 Youth hostel

● The route

The vertical photography used in the photo-maps is taken from an average height above sea level. This means that the scale of the photography will alter slightly as the contours of the ground vary. The photo-maps are constructed by piecing together a series of photographs to make each page. They are intended to give a

he Route

nd 'Offa's Dyke Path' - attached to stiles and posts.
   Wye Valley Walk: Although well-maintained and early marked with yellow arrows, the route is complex nd summer growth can obscure some of the waymarks.

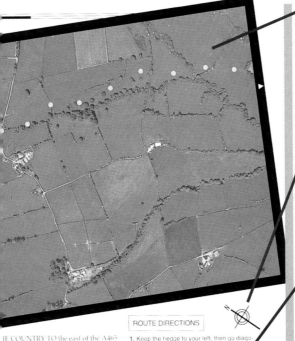

VERTICAL PHOTO-MAPS
The path is plotted on vertical photographs using a scale of 1:10,000 (0.6 miles:3.9ins, 1km:10cm).

COMPASS POINT
Every photo-map is accompanied by a compass point for ease of orientation.

ROUTE DIRECTIONS
These numbered route directions correspond to the numbers shown in yellow on the photo-maps.

GENERAL TEXT
Places to visit, points of specific interest and information relevant to each stretch of the route accompanies the photo-maps. Always check opening times of places to visit in advance. Generally, opening times between October and Easter are very limited.

SCALE FOR PHOTO-MAPS
The scale-bar represents a distance of 0.310 miles (0.5km).

ROUTE DIRECTIONS

IE COUNTRY TO the east of the A465 rather bland in contrast with the high d wild ground of the Black Mountains. oking back from the vicinity of merch at (2), the eastern escarpment of Hatterrall can be seen running to the rth above the Olchon valley as far as distant prow of the Cat's Back Ridge d the Black Hill.
To the south lies the distinctive hinx-like mass of Ysgyryd Fawr, 'the ridge'. This hill, known colloquially The Skirrid (1,594ft/486m), has an ea of landslip on its north-western oulder, a feature caused by the same assive slippage of a sandstone mass on bricated marl as seen at Black Darren d above Cwmyoy. Legend would have otherwise, of course, with local stories aiming that the feature was caused by a dden earth movement at the time of e crucifixion of Christ, or that the notch as where Noah's Ark grounded.
The Skirrid certainly has the natural yle of a 'Holy Mountain' and was nsidered as such for many years. There e vestigial ruins of a small chapel on e summit. This chapel, probably edieval, was a place of pilgrimage until e 17th century. The main mass of The kirrid was given to the National Trust

1. Keep the hedge to your left, then go diagonally right across the next field to stiles and plank over a ditch. Go diagonally left across a field, just to the left of a wooded gully, and continue on to another stile and plank bridge. Continue straight ahead to stiles and a plank bridge, then keep to the highest part of the next field, before going half-left to reach a road.
2. Turn left up the road and go right at the T-junction. After 100yds turn left into the drive to Llanerch. Walk up the drive and go through a gate and down the left side of two fields to go over a stile in the left corner of the second field to a road.
3. Turn left for 100yds, then go right over a stile by a stream. Continue to a stile under a huge oak, then pass a ruined building and keep on a distinct path to a stile. Continue straight ahead over a rise.

in 1939. The hill can be reached by keeping south for a mile (1.6km) on the lane (A) leading past the left turn into the drive to Llanerch.
This is the last of mountainous Wales for walkers on the Offa's Dyke Path. Southwards, there comes a sense of plunging into a pastoral maze of fields and spinneys, of innumerable crossings of tiny streams and sodden ditches through a fertile landscape drained by the Full Brook and the River Trothy.

pictorial representation of the ground and strict accuracy of scale throughout cannot be guaranteed. There may also be a mismatch in areas of extreme relief – ie where the land is steepest. These problems have been kept to a minimum, in particular close to the main route of the walk.

OFFA'S DYKE PATH

THIS GUIDE DESCRIBES in detail the southern section of the Offa's Dyke Path from Knighton to Sedbury on the banks of the Severn, a distance of 80 miles (128km). The complete Offa's Dyke Path is 177 miles (285km) long. It was established in 1971 by the Countryside Commission in conjunction with the various county councils for the districts through which the route passes. The fabric of the route, including stiles and signposts, is maintained in excellent condition. Much of the work is carried out by dedicated volunteers, not least from the Offa's Dyke Association which has been closely associated with the path from its conception.

Following the route in its entirety is a tough, though rewarding, undertaking. Walkers should be well equipped for extremes of conditions in the Hergest Ridge area and in the Black Mountains where the weather can be severe. There are a number of youth hostels and camp sites on or near the route, and hotels and bed- and-breakfast establishments are plentiful around the towns and larger villages.

Walkers should be aware that not all sections of the path are public rights of way; some are permissive paths through private property.

The 8th-century earthwork is a unique 'ancient monument' that extends through the Welsh borders. It was built by Offa, King of Mercia, as part of a border which ran for 150 miles (240km) from modern Prestatyn on the north coast of Wales to the River Severn. It marked out the disputed north-south line between Celtic Wales and Saxon Mercia, incorporating natural boundaries of high hills and areas of inpenetrable forest.

The bank-and-ditch formation has survived unbroken over substantial distances, though much has been lost to agriculture, rural development and natural erosion. What remains ranges from vestigal stretches of grassy or tree-crowned bank to substantial embankments 20ft (6m) in height.

It is the linear though fragmented nature of the Dyke that makes the tracing of much of its course via the modern

Left: The Kymin, near Monmouth

Below left: Oswestry Fort

Right: The Vale of Ewyas

Below: The village of Clyro, near Ross-on-Wye

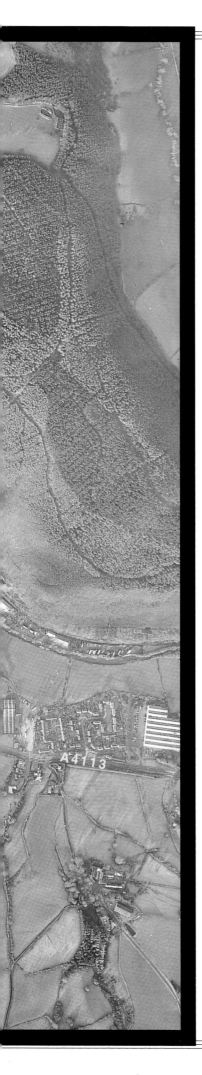

Knighton to Ditchyeld

9 miles (14.4km)

The southern half of the Offa's Dyke Path starts at Knighton. From here the path leading south to Dolley Green and Ditchyeld introduces the walker to several impressive sections of the Dyke as it runs through typically fine border country. The going is reasonable, with only a few steep sections.

ROUTE DIRECTIONS

1. Turn left into West Street from the Offa's Dyke Centre. Go down past the clock-tower and on down Broad Street. Cross the road and turn right through the archway of the Knighton Hotel. Go directly across a car park (public lavatories – closed from 6pm) then continue up Larket Lane opposite.

2. At the top of Larket Lane turn right into Ffrydd Road, then immediately cross the road with care to go up a short lane between houses. Turn right, continue in front of some garages, then veer left up a path. Cross a surfaced lane and follow the left-hand of two paths steeply uphill and through the woods. (Offa's Dyke appears down on the right as a low bank running parallel to the path.)

3. Go over a stile, then bear right along by a fence with a golf course on your left. The path is firm under foot but can be quite muddy in places.

KNIGHTON LIES AT the heart of the Welsh border country, handsomely situated amidst wooded hills on a rise above the River Teme.

Now a typical market town, Knighton evolved from early settlement patterns, as nearby Iron Age hill forts show. Important during the Mercian period as a defensive and administrative centre, Knighton became firmly established in the 11th century with the building of a Norman castle, of which little remains. A stroll along Knighton's High Street and round the upper town is rewarding.

There are numerous well-stocked shops in the town, as well as several hotels and pubs, restaurants and cafés plus a good choice of accommodation raging from the youth hostel at the Offa's Dyke Centre to hotels, guesthouses and bed-and-breakfast establishments. There is a railway station, too, which although unstaffed, has timetables prominently displayed. Connections can be made to Shrewsbury and to Llandrindod Wells.

Offa's Dyke leads south through Knighton then skirts the west side of the town

OFFA'S DYKE becomes dramatically higher where the path bears right (1). The overall height from the base of the ditch to the top of the bank is about 60ft (18m) and it is thought that a different work gang may have operated from this point. The Dyke here is covered with trees and is nicely dark and atmospheric. Some way down its length there is a clear, though narrow gap with a farm gate on its east side. This passageway allowed the movement of Welsh drovers and others to be controlled by the Mercians and was probably aligned with an existing east-west track way that led from the Welsh interior to the Plain of Hereford, emphasising the administrative nature of Offa's Dyke, rather than its military significance. The Mercian's desire to control trade across the Welsh Marches reflects the new territorial interests which developed during the Saxon era and indicated a significant cultural and political advance towards greater stability.

Beyond the traffic gap, where the path leads through fields to reach the minor road of Woodhouse Lane at Dyke House, the Dyke reduces in height once more. To the west lies Rhos Hill. Physical evidence of the Dyke is lost here, suggesting its destruction by later road and farming developments. The line continues directly from the Dyke House area through fields but the walker must make a detour by road to regain the Dyke path from the B4355.

The path cutting a corner of the B4355 (3) runs along the top of the Dyke for some distance. There is a large east ditch and lesser west ditch along the first part of this section, although the Dyke soon becomes lower and indistinct. The path can be pleasantly overgrown; in places the twisted roots of trees snake across the surface amidst a wealth of wild flowers such as harebell, pignut, purple loosestrife, and stitchwort. The 19th century waymark stone by the roadside at the end of this section records the 'making' of Offa's Dyke as 757. This may reflect careless dating by the road-builders, since the Dyke was built between 778 and 796. The year 757 was the start of Offa's reign.

ROUTE DIRECTIONS

1. Bear right through a break where the Dyke becomes much higher. Turn left and continue down the edges of several fields with the Dyke on your left. Go through a narrow section of scrub and on through fields and over stiles to reach a road at Rhos-y-meirch. **2.** Turn left at the road, then left again on to the B4357 and pass a telephone box. Go right at the junction with the B4355 and continue up the road for a ¼ mile (400m) to a point just past a house on the right. **3.** Cross the road, with care, and go over a stile in the hedge. Turn right and follow a path along the Dyke to rejoin the B4355 at Offa's Stone, a 19th century waymarker. The path along this section can become overgrown.

N

RHOS-Y-MEIRCH

B4357

① ② ③

ROUTE DIRECTIONS

1. Cross the B4355 and go over a stile on to some rough ground. Follow the line of a fence and trees for about l00yds, then bear left through a break in the gorse to reach a farm track. Turn right, then, beyond a stile, bear left and go up a path through some gorse, passing a reedy pond on the right. Follow a muddy path into a field. There is a prominent monument in the centre of the field. Bear right and follow the path alongside a conifer plantation.

2. Follow the distinctive line of Offa's Dyke across the airy heights of Hawthorn Hill, 1335ft (407m).

3. When descending Hawthorn Hill, turn sharp right beyond a stile and after l50yds turn sharp left. Continue downhill along a grassy track.

N

WHITTON

B4356

THE MOST STRIKING feature at the beginning of this section is the rather incongruous and lonely monument that stands in the middle of a field close to where the path crosses Cwm Whitton Hill. The monument, of polished red granite, was erected in memory of the 19th century baronet, Sir Richard Green Price (1803-1887), MP for Radnor Borough and later Radnor. Sir Richard campaigned vigorously to have the railway extended to Knighton and on to Landrindod Wells, and from Leominster to Kington, Presteigne and New Radnor. The advantages of 19th century rail links within this isolated border region were great. Unfortunately the monument was damaged by gales in the mid-1970s, but it has been restored.

The path (2) follows the line of Offa's Dyke across Hawthorn Hill, with fine views to the hills of the Radnor Forest in the west and to Herrock Hill and the Hergest Ridge in the south and the Black Mountains beyond. Offa's Dyke rather wanders across this open area which has led to speculation that the 8th century engineers had to navigate their way through what was then dense woodland, now long gone.

The presence of a ditch on the Mercian east side seems inexplicable; it may have resulted from the whim or misunderstanding of a particular construction gang. The sense of the Dyke's dominant position between Wales and Mercia is emphasised south of Hawthorn Hill's summit where the Dyke becomes indistinct. Here the path skirts the rim of the steep northern slope of Gilfach Hill, passing above the narrow cwm that plunges dramatically to Gilfach Farm. Beyond here the path begins its descent from Furrow Hill towards the lovely valley of the River Lugg.

Pen Offa Hill, to the west of the path

ROUTE DIRECTIONS

1. Bear left at a signpost, just before a conifer plantation.

2. Cross a stile by a sheep fold and follow a stony track downhill to reach the B4356 at Dolley Green. Go right along the road for 250yds.

3. Bear down left and through a gate. Continue down the left-hand edge of a field to cross Dolley Old Bridge over the River Lugg. Follow the river for a short distance and continue in the same line from where the river bends upstream. Go alongside a hawthorn hedge through two fields to reach a road. The hamlet of Discoed lies 400yds to the left.

4. Go over the stile on the opposite side of the road. Follow the path on a moderately steep climb along the crest of Offa's Dyke, which is very distinct but diminishes towards the top of the rising ground. Descend, with a hawthorn hedge on the right, to reach the road at Bwlch.

5. Go over a stile on the opposite side of the road, then continue

across a field on the obvious line of the Dyke passing a 'traffic' gap. When level with Pen Offa Farm on the right, go over a stile next to an iron gate, and continue along the Dyke and into the conifers of Hilltop Plantation.

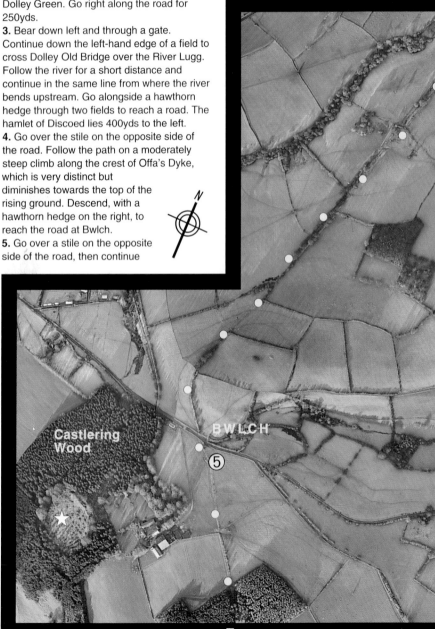

Castlering Wood

BWLCH

⑤

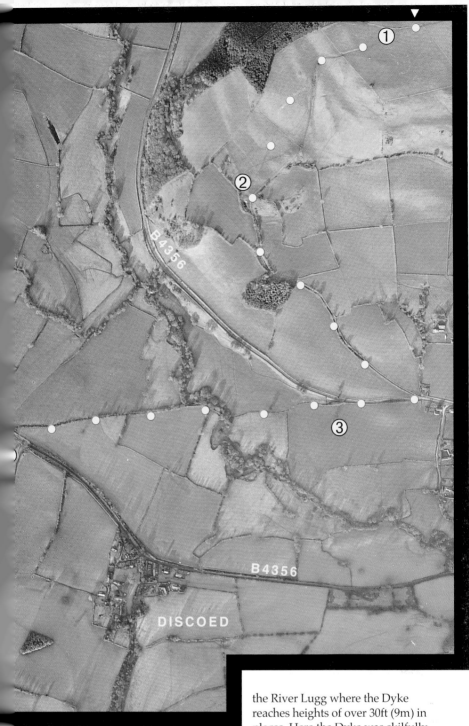

THE LINE OF Offa's Dyke has been lost where it once crossed the valley floor of the River Lugg, but its substantial size and straight alignment up the southern slope convinced Cyril Fox that the valley slopes of the 8th century were cultivable, and probably cleared of trees, with a sharp transition to forested upland at higher levels. Fox cites the change in the Dyke's alignment from straight to irregular at the 900-ft (273m) contour line above Discoed as an indication that here the Dyke builders left clear ground and moved into the wooded upland.

The walker enjoys a powerful impression of the original Offa's Dyke and its purpose on the way south from the River Lugg where the Dyke reaches heights of over 30ft (9m) in places. Here the Dyke was skilfully engineered on the rise from the valley to ensure a clear overview of the western approach from Wales. At Bwlch, meaning 'pass' or 'gap', the modern road to Presteigne passes along an ancient ridgeway leading east from the Welsh fastness of Radnor Forest. A short distance south-east of the road there is evidence of a 'border control' traffic gap through Offa's Dyke. The ridgeway route may have been blocked off at the present road's position and travellers made to divert through the control gap at this strategic point.

Just west of the path above Bwlch, in Castlering Wood, lies the site of an Iron Age hillfort, possibly aligned to the much larger Burfa Bank fort 2 miles (3.2km) to the south.

EVENJOBB

① ② ③ ④

Bur
Farmhous

THE ATTRACTIVE TOWN of
Presteigne lies 2 miles (3.2km) east of
Dolley Green along the B4356.
Presteigne can also be reached along
the minor roads crossed by the Offa's
Dyke Path on its way south to
Ditchyeld Bridge. Presteigne's Welsh-
ness is essentially territorial. The
town lies at the confluence of the
River Lugg and the Hindwell Brook
where the the national border thrusts
into England. The town's Welsh
name is Llanandras, after St
Andrew's Church, a mainly 14th century building which is a pleasing
example of the perpendicular style of
late Gothic architecture.

Presteigne's Saxon name was *Pres-
themede*, 'the household of priests',

recalling a 10th century religious foundation and an 'Englishness' which remained intact through centuries of border dispute. A Norman motte and bailey was established on high ground above the town. Thereafter, Presteigne flourished as a market town and cloth manufactury for many centuries, despite ravages by intermittent plague and by the Welsh champions, Gruffyd ap Llywelyn (1052), Llywelyn the Great (1213) and Owain Glyndwr (1401). Presteigne was the county town of the former county of Radnorshire and although it has declined in strategic and commercial importance it retains a strong sense of identity and border charm. The town is well supplied with shops, pubs, hotels, eating places and varied accommodation. There are banks, a post office, and a tourist information centre. Bus services connect with Leominster.

The stretch of Offa's Dyke Path from Hilltop Plantation to the valley of the Hindwell Brook at Ditchyeld maintains close contact with the Dyke itself. The path also affords exhilarating views from the high ground it traverses. To the south, the walker can see the immediate features of Granner Wood, Knill Wood and Burfa Bank. Beyond lies Herrock Hill and Rushock Hill with the Hergest Ridge in the far distance. To the west lie the wooded heights of the Forest of Radnor with its high points of Black Mixen and Great Rhos.

ROUTE DIRECTIONS

1. A steady climb leads up through Hilltop Plantation to the hill's summit, then descends to bear right through the Dyke and down to cross a stile at the edge of some woodland. Continue across a field alongside the low-hedged Dyke on the left, then descend very steeply to join a track by a farm shed. Go left along the track for 100yds.
2. Turn right off the track and go down a grass track. Keep left at a fork, then go into a conifer plantation. Follow the track through woods and cross a forestry road. Go down steps, then turn left along a muddy path on top of the Dyke. Go right down wooden steps to bear left over a stile and on to a narrow lane. The hamlet of Evenjobb, where there is a post office and telephone, is ½ mile (800m) west along this lane.
3. Cross the lane and go up steps and over a stile. Continue through fields and over stiles following the line of the Dyke to where the path goes down right to reach a road.
4. Go left along the road for 50yds, then go right along a track past farmhouse buildings, and the medieval Burfa Farmhouse on the left.

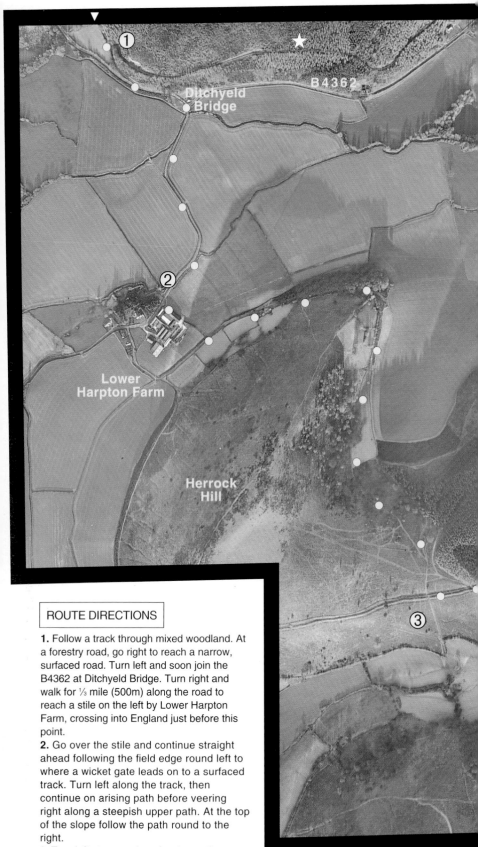

Ditchyeld Bridge

B4362

① ② ③

Lower Harpton Farm

Herrock Hill

ROUTE DIRECTIONS

1. Follow a track through mixed woodland. At a forestry road, go right to reach a narrow, surfaced road. Turn left and soon join the B4362 at Ditchyeld Bridge. Turn right and walk for ⅓ mile (500m) along the road to reach a stile on the left by Lower Harpton Farm, crossing into England just before this point.

2. Go over the stile and continue straight ahead following the field edge round left to where a wicket gate leads on to a surfaced track. Turn left along the track, then continue on arising path before veering right along a steepish upper path. At the top of the slope follow the path round to the right.

3. Turn left at a crossing of paths on the saddle of Herrock Hill, 1,217ft (371m). Join a track, then go over a stile by a gate and continue along the track with the Dyke on the right. Walkers should avoid walking on the crest of the Dyke along this section because of erosion to the bank. Swing right at a right-angled corner in the Dyke on the flat summit of Rushock Hill, 1,244ft (379m). After 400yds turn sharp right and follow a grassy groove down the field.

4. Continue alongside a line of old apple trees on the left. Go over the next stile and bear left to the far corner of a larch plantation. Go over another stile and pass a handsome oak tree. Continue straight ahead and uphill.

Ditchyeld to Newchurch

12 miles (19.2km)

This next section of the Offa's Dyke Path runs south through splendid hill country via Herrock Hill and Rushock Hill and on down to Kington. The path then abandons the line of the Dyke for the airy heights of the Hergest Ridge, descending to Gladestry before climbing over Disgwylfa Hill to Newchurch. There are some lengthy ups and downs, but the walking is generally reasonable and very rewarding.

ON BURFA HILL, to the north of Ditchyeld Bridge, lie the remains of Burfa Camp, a large Iron Age hill fort of 20 acres (8ha). One of the largest of the great border camps, the site is now surrounded by trees.

Once on the saddle of Herrock Hill, the view to the south opens up towards Bradnor Hill in the immediate foreground with the Hergest Ridge in the distance. From the high point of Rushock Hill the views are panoramic, north-east to the Malverns, east across the Plain of Hereford, south-east to the Wye valley, and south to the Black Mountains and the Brecons.

Herrock Hill and Rushock Hill make up the last highland area traversed by Offa's Dyke. It is here, too, that the Dyke and long-distance path diverge. The walker will not meet with the Dyke again until south of Monmouth.

Bradnor
Hill

① ②

④

Hergest
Croft

1. Cross the middle of a field to the edge of a wood. Go right to a stile by a gate, then cross a field keeping to the right above a house. A surfaced track leads to a lane where a right turn gains the road below Bradnor Hill, which is partly occupied by a golf course.

2. Go diagonally left across the road and descend a sunken track over the fairway of the golf course (watch out for golf balls). Pass a cottage on the left and reach the open space of Bradnor Green. Continue to the left of a cottage to reach a wicket gate between whitewashed cottages. Go down the hedge-enclosed path and on through a variety of gates to reach a steep sunken lane where a left turn leads to the busy A44.

3. Cross the main road, with care, then cross a footbridge over the Back Brook. Turn left and walk up Crooked Well Lane. Go directly ahead at a crossroads and then bear right past the old National School building. Go left across the open space of Common Close and turn right into the Square. Go right by the Swan Inn into Church Street. (The centre of Kington is down left.) Follow Church Street uphill to reach the lych-gate of the Church of St Mary the Virgin.

4. Pass the entrance to the church and continue through the churchyard to go down a lane between houses. Cross the main road (with care) and follow a footpath on the left side of a narrow lane directly opposite. Follow the steep Ridgebourne Road past Hergest Croft Gardens (open daily, Easter to end of October 1.30pm to 6.30 pm).

KINGTON LIES ON the banks of the River Arrow between the Welsh hills and the English plain and combines the traditional qualities of Herefordshire and old Radnorshire. The town is believed to be named after Edward the Confessor, although an earlier form of its 'royal town' status was reflected in the name 'Chingtune', a possible Saxon link to Offa himself. Kington retains its later medieval pattern of narrow streets forming grid lines on either side of a

museum repays a visit.

A visit to the Church of St Mary the Virgin should be irresistible to the walker since the Offa's Dyke Path diverts past the rather fine 18th century lych-gate and the church door. St Mary's is a handsome church; its 12th century tower was detached at one time and may have been as much for defensive as sacred use. The graceful spire mounted on truncated pyramids, or broaches, is 18th century. The interior of the church

central high street. It was a thriving market and manufacturing town for centuries, linked to the South Wales coal mines and iron works by a horse-drawn tram railway in the early 19th century. Modern Kington retains much of its traditional style in spite of heavy-handed Victorian restoration of some of its buildings. The town

is spacious and elegant and there are several notable features, including the alabaster tomb of the 15th century Thomas Vaughan and his wife, Ellen Gethin.

Kington has numerous shops and other facilities including banks, a post office and a tourist information centre. There are also plenty of pubs, hotels, restaurants and cafés.

The Whetstone

③

Old Race Course

HERGEST RIDGE (pronounced Hargest) makes for an exhilarating walk, although it can be wild and inhospitable when Welsh weather streams in from the west. The series of marker posts alongside low way marks is a reminder, during fine summer weather, that Hergest can be smothered in snow in winter. Equally, the Hergest Ridge can be quite daunting during a mid-summer storm and walkers should be well-prepared at all times. From the airy heights of Hergest the view to the north-west reveals the Vale of Radnor, a distinctive region enfolded within the hills of Radnor Forest with their high tops of Black Mixen and Great Rhos.

The 'old' race course, established in 1826, has not been used for many years. Prior to this there was a race course on Bradnor Hill to the north. It is believed that during the 17th and 18th centuries, before horse-racing became a feature of the late 18th century, races on foot had been a popular custom on Bradnor Hill: our modern passion for keep-fit and athletics may be nothing new.

The Kington Races, usually held in July and August, were substantial affairs. There is an original race card of August 1841 in Kington's excellent

museum which gives a true flavour of such events.

The small plantation of Chile pines (monkey puzzle trees) on the summit of Hergest is intriguing. They were planted in the late 1980s by the owner of Hergest Croft, probably as an interesting experiment.

North-west of Hergest lies Old Radnor. There was once a castle here and the area featured in border history for centuries. During the Civil War of the 17th century Charles I stayed at Old Radnor after his retreat from the Battle of Naseby.

The town is now distinguished by its church with its handsome tower and 14th century windows. The church's font is of great antiquity and may have been carved from a Bronze Age stone like those at nearby Kinnerton.

ROUTE DIRECTIONS

1. The steep lane becomes a rough track after 3⁄4 mile (1.2km) and leads to a gate on to the open moorland of Hergest Ridge. Do not follow the track that bears right; instead, continue on a broad grassy track keeping a line of trees and a hedge to the left.

2. Keep ahead on the broad grassy track when the line of trees bends away to the left.

3. Cross the distinctive track of the Kington race course and continue in a westerly direction on a grassy track along the broad-backed ridge. Pass a small planting of monkey-puzzle trees, then cross the western arm of the old Kington race course. (The glacial erratic boulder known as The Whetstone is a short distance round to the right from this point.)

THE PATH (2) descends gently on close-cropped turf which becomes swathed in bracken during the autumn. This is bare windswept country, grazed by sheep and colonised by the hardiest of mountain plants. In the turfy hollows of the path the wettest areas of grass are an emerald green. There is a dramatic contrast on the final descent from the ridge where the surfaced lane leading down towards Gladestry is flanked by a hedgerow of mixed shrubs, including wild damsons, beech, privet, hawthorn, holly, gorse and elder. At the bottom of the lane, the frothy white blossoms of Russian vine contrast with the ivy-draped wall of Elm Villa.

Gladestry is an attractive little village on the banks of the Gladestry Brook. It is overlooked by the shapely Yewtree Bank – the western spur of Hergest Ridge. There is a post office/shop in the village

and the Royal Oak Inn is a welcome stopping off place for weary travellers.

Just under a mile (1km) to the north-west lies Court of Gladestry, once the home of Sir Gelli Meyrick, an Elizabethan owner of Radnor Forest. Meyrick was one of about 300 supporters of Robert Devereux, the Earl of Essex who, in 1601, failed in his attempt at a *coup d'état* which included a planned kidnapping of the ageing Queen Elizabeth. Courtiers like Meyrick shared Devereux's sense of bitterness against the Elizabethan court under Secretary of State, Sir Robert Cecil. Perhaps Meyrick should have stayed in Radnor. Like Essex and many others, he was executed for his recklessness.

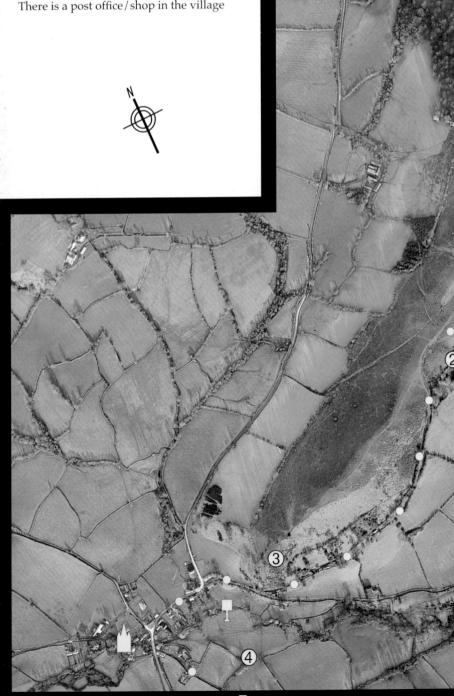

ROUTE DIRECTIONS

1. Continue on the gentle descent from the top of the ridge, then cross back into Wales along the left-hand grassy track where tracks diverge by two dark-leaved rowan trees. Pass another pond on the right and continue on a gradual descent.

2. Keep on the main path to reach a dip before the distinctive knoll of Yewtree Bank. Do not continue on the path leading over Yewtree Bank, but instead, from the dip, bear round to the left and go down a path leading to a stile by a gate. Continue past a house and on down a surfaced lane.

3. At the bottom of the lane turn right along a road, then turn left into Gladestry. Pass the Royal Oak Inn and continue along the B4594 for 250yds, passing the Church of St Mary on the right.

4. Turn left along a narrow lane for ½ mile (800m).

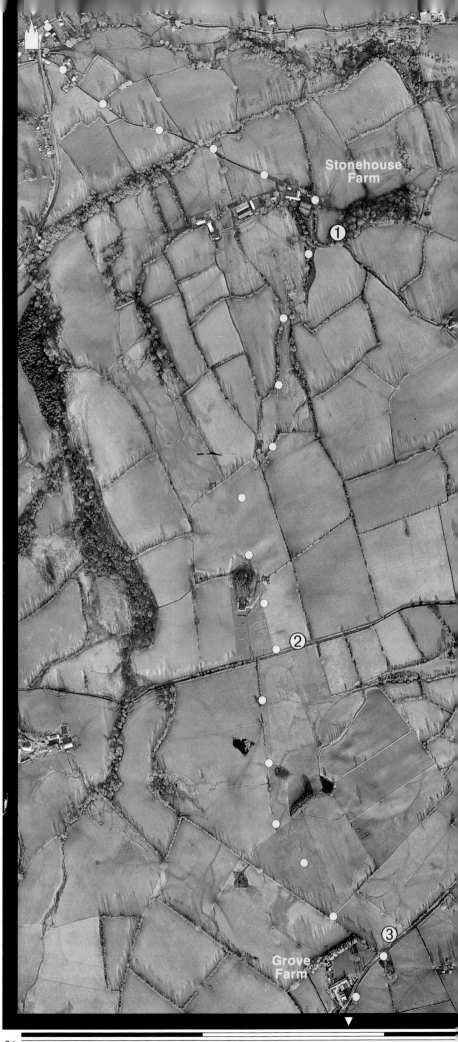

Stonehouse
Farm

①

②

③

Grove
Farm

The remains of Huntington Castle, lying practically on the Welsh border

THE LANE THAT runs from Gladestry to Stonehouse Farm seems almost incapable of accommodating vehicles, it is so narrow. The section of path beyond here runs through typical border country with the national border itself never too far away. But the path remains steadfastly in Wales, only brushing England near Grove Farm.

This was a contested land, not least during the Norman era. The Norman Conquest of Britain was of seminal importance in the nation's development as the Normans, although a warrior breed, had great political sophistication. However, like other invaders, they attempted to dispossess reigning chieftains and Norman castles sprang up along the Marches. The armed aggressiveness of the Norman system contrasted with Offa's day when the Anglo-Saxons and the Welsh were at least moving towards some form of graceful compromise, with Offa's Dyke representing a political rather than a military boundary. Yet resistance was vigorous from Wales, and Norman militarism became self-perpetuating. Castle-building in the Marches went on for four centuries and the Norman achievement was to define, brutally, the racial and cultural divide between English and Welsh. The Norman failure was an inability to subjugate Wales.

East of this section of the Offa's Dyke Path lies the site of Huntington Castle, a classic example of the Norman motte and bailey construction. The original site may

well have been an earlier Anglo-Saxon settlement. The Norman remains date from the early 13th century and represent what was a round keep on a raised platform, the motte. There would have been a curtain wall enclosing an inner bailey or yard, with an outer bailey attached.

ROUTE DIRECTIONS

1. Just past Stonehouse Farm, go right over a stile and up a track. Cross a stream and continue up a slope on the right. Bear left along a track, then join a wider track. Go through a gate and over a stile, and stay left alongside a field hedge. Go right along another field hedge. Go over a wooden stile in the bottom corner of the field, with Stone House Barn to the right. Continue between wire fencing to reach a road.

2. Turn right along the road then go left into an area of open, rolling fields. Keep the hedge to your right. Go over a second stile and bear diagonally left to reach the edge of a stand of conifers. Continue, keeping a fence to your right, to reach a road.

3. Turn right (with your heel pivoting for a mere second on the Welsh-English border), then just after passing Grove Farm on the right, go left on to a surfaced track. Go past Hill House, where, on the wall of a barn, there is a tap for thirsty travellers. An accompanying poem by R. Kinsey-Croose invites walkers to slake their thirst. Continue along the track, which becomes rough, then go over a stile on to the open hillside of Disgwylfa Hill. In 200yds, at a junction, fork right and climb steadily up a wide green track.

Newchurch to Hay-on-Wye

6 ½ miles (10.4km)

South of Newchurch the route winds its way through some lovely border country along paths and country lanes from where views to the Black Hills and across the Wye valley are impressive. The going is varied and easy.

ROUTE DIRECTIONS

1. Continue over the path's high point on Dis-gwylfa Hill (1,260ft/384m), then descend gently to pass a pond on the right. The way is not obvious over this next section. Continue over short turfy moorland, bearing right over the brow of the hill ahead to reach a white signpost. Continue down the slope to another signpost, then descend very steeply to pick up a field hedge on the left. Reach a gate on to a track which is followed to the B4594 at Newchurch.

2. Turn left along the road and cross the River Arrow (telephone kiosk on the right). Go left past St Mary's Church and on to the Michaelchurch road. After 100yds, where the road bears left, leave the road and go ahead along a narrow unsurfaced track (no through road sign) for a ⅓ mile (500m) to where the track bends sharply right towards Gilfach-yr-heol Farm.

3. Go ahead off the road and along a short section of green lane, which can be very muddy. Go through a gate, turn right, then bear up left and follow a track across open ground. Continue across the flank of Little Mountain over stiles and keeping a hedge on the left. Go through some gorse bushes at a field corner to a stile into a green lane.

Little Mountain

★ Roman Camp

Disgwylfa Hill (meaning 'watching place') is an
exhilarating viewpoint in good weather

① Pen Twyn

② Cae-Higgen Farm

③ Llwyngwilliam Farm

Pen Twyn Camp, an ancient settlement just east of the Dyke

THE ROUTE NOW follows the line of an ancient track way to join country lanes on the way to the banks of the River Wye. The short section of track (1) is probably on the line of a very old route that led east and west along a ridgeway. The route would have pre-dated its Roman use which the Little Mountain encampment indicates. It was probably Bronze Age and possibly earlier. The tree-shrouded green lane which is followed after the first road junction is a particular delight. It is bordered on the west by an ancient drystone wall and the views westwards into Wales reveal the elegant lines of the border hills of Bryng-wyn and Red Hill.

Just over a mile (1.6km) west of the path near the ancient settlement of Dolbedwen are the tree-shrouded remains of a Norman motte fortification, another of the typical castle mounds of the Marcher lords. A few hundred yards to the east lie the remnants of Pen Twyn settlement, an Iron Age feature. The Roman site at Little Mountain underlines the strategic importance of this area throughout hundreds of years

of territorial struggle. Looking south from the route (2) above Cae-Higgin, the view to the Black Mountains and the wide sweep of the Wye valley is exhilarating.

A mile (1.6km) east along the road from (3) is the village of Rhydspence with its ancient inn dating from the mid-14th century. Rhydspence had two inns for many centuries, the present one being on the English side of the border, the other on the Welsh side. The Welsh inn is now a private house. Both inns were very busy during the great days of the drovers who brought their sturdy hill cattle out of Wales on the long haul to Kent. The English inn was also a smithy, a facility much needed by the drovers since their cattle were shod with small iron 'cues' to cope with the wear and tear of travel. The drovers were also the news-gatherers and carriers of their day, often entrusted with making financial transactions in London. The road running west from (3) leads to another droving village, Painscastle, which had its own drovers' inn and forge.

ROUTE DIRECTIONS

1. Keep right at a junction and continue down a lane along the precise line of the national boundary. Reach a surfaced continuation road and pass into England just before a T-junction with another road. At the T-junction go ahead through a gate and continue along a green lane, which can be very muddy and wet. Reach a road and turn left.
2. In about 500yds, cross into Wales once

again and then, by Cae-Higgen Farm, go over a stile in a hedge on the right and bear left across a field to a stile into another field. Continue in the same line to rejoin the road just before a house.
3. Turn right along the road for just under ½ mile (800m) to reach a crossroads. Llwyngwilliam Farm lies up to the right. Go left down a narrow lane.

Bettws Dingle

① ②

ROUTE DIRECTIONS

1. A ⅓ mile (500m) along the descending lane from the turn by Llwyngwilliam Farm, reach a dip in the lane amidst trees. Turn off left and go down some steps. After 300yds go right, down a stony and muddy track, to cross Cabalfa Brook. It is usually very muddy here except in the driest conditions.

2. Go up steeply and continue down to the left of an old barn. Follow the path above the deep, wooded ravine of Bettws Dingle. Bear up right away from the track when abreast of Cwm-bwllfa's ruined farm up on the right. Go over a

stile and continue along the path. Turn right on to a track, then soon bear left and join a surfaced road which leads to the right and steeply downhill to the main A438. Turn right and walk, with care, along the road for about 400yds.

3. Cross the road, with care, and go over a stile, then bear down to the right. Continue along the path then go left across a concrete bridge over a stream. Bear right through two fields to keep left of a large barn. Bear right and continue across fields. Keep towards the right edge of a final field, then go over a stile and turn left along a green lane.

Hay, with a typically violent border history between the Welsh and the English, couldn't be more peaceful today

THERE ARE DRAMATIC changes in landscape on this section of the path, especially between the sudden descent from wooded upland to the broad, flat meadows of the River Wye. The first part of the route leads through the gloomy pines of Bettws Dingle, providing welcome shade in hot summer weather but otherwise dark and gothic. Conifer plantations are bereft of rich plant life, so dark and sunless is the under-storey of the woodland floor. This is rich ground for fungi, however, examples being the the thin-capped tawny grisette or the plump blusher with its reddish-brown cap and white speckles. No fungi should be eaten unless expert advice is available.

Once through the long tunnel of pines (1) the rutted and stony track drops down to the wet floor of the valley of the Cabalfa Brook. The name 'cabalfa' means 'place of the ferry' and refers probably to the point where the brook joins the River Wye below Cabalva Farm. It is likely that there was once a ferry here in ancient times.

Crossing the busy A438 (3) comes as something of a shock after the quiet countryside. Another contrast comes with the flat river fields of the Wye. From the edge of the road, the muddy waters of the river coil across the flat ground ahead. Beyond the river valley, the way ahead is dominated by the high ground of Hay Bluff and the Hatterrall Ridge of the Black Mountains. Ahead lies Hay-on-Wye.

Hay-on-Wye to Hay Bluff

5 miles (6.4km)

The section of the Offa's Dyke Path described here is kept purposefully short. The upland section of the route beyond the Gospel Road comprises 13 miles (20.8km) of high-level walking before Pandy is reached. Some walkers may not wish to undertake this in bad weather. There is an alternative route by road from Gospel Pass through the Vale of Ewyas.

WHERE THE PATH reaches the banks of the River Wye (1) it is overlooked by the site of what was a very large Roman enclosure of 26 acres (10.5ha). There may have been forts on the site at different periods.

The attractive village of Clyro lies a mile (1.6km) to the north-west of Hay-on-Wye. Clyro is where Francis Kilvert served as a curate for seven years and began his illuminating diaries. The village can be reached by turning right at (2) and going along the B4351.

Hay-on-Wye is situated on high ground with the River Wye to the north and the great bastion of the Black Mountains to the south and west. In spite of some modernisation, it retains its pleasing layout clustered round the remnants of a Norman 'castle' with its grafted-on 17th century structure. There are narrow winding streets with distinctive features like the town clock and the collonaded butter market.

However, it is Hay's remarkable status in the second-hand book trade which lends it a special fascination. There are 20 major bookshops in the town and even part of the castle houses a bookseller. Walkers who are addictive browsers run the risk of never getting back on to the south-bound path.

Hay has a number of shops and other facilities such as banks and a post office. There is a tourist information office above the large car park near where the Offa's Dyke Path leaves the town. There is also a range of accommodation here, and a number of good pubs, restaurants and cafés.

ROUTE DIRECTIONS

1. Where the lane bends sharply right, go left through a field gate, turning immediately right along the edge of a long field. Continue straight ahead through fields, bearing right to the banks of the Wye. Continue along the river bank, then go up a muddy path and along a section that is overhung with holly and hawthorn. Go up steps and on to the B4351.

2. Turn left across Clyro Bridge and go along Bridge Street. Turn right along Broad Street opposite a flower-filled horse trough, a memorial to a local stock-dealer. Fork left by the clock-tower and cross the road to bear left up The Pavement, a cobbled walkway. Turn right into Hightown, then go left across Castle Square and continue into the narrow Castle Lane below the castle. Turn right to reach the main road. Cross the road and go down the narrow lane obliquely opposite between curving walls.

3. Take the left-hand one of two kissing-gates and follow the path through two fields, keeping the hedge on your left. Dogs should be kept on leads in these fields. Go through another kissing-gate into a field and keep the fence on the right to reach a third kissing-gate. Continue straight on to the next kissing-gate.

River
Wye

Roman Fort

① ② ③

HAY-ON-WYE

P

ROUTE DIRECTIONS

1. Continue alongside Cusop Dingle to cross a wooden bridge called, inevitably, the Kissing Bridge, or, in Welsh, *Y Pont Gusanu*. Cusop House is on the left. Ascend about 50yds to go over a stile and continue to a yew tree at the corner of a copse, then go diagonally right across a field to reach a lane. Turn left and go up the lane for 400yds.

2. Turn right at a wooden signpost by the second gate on the right and continue uphill. The stream is on you right. Cross a footbridge when opposite a house on the left, then continue over stiles to the farm track of Upper Dan-y-Fforest.

3. Go left on the farm track then right over a stile to continue very steeply up a field towards a holly tree. At the holly tree go right into an upper field. Go left and continue steeply to a stile on to a rough lane.

4. Turn left past Cadwgan Farm. The stony track beyond here can be very wet at times. Reach a gate on to the open moors.

N

Long Cairn

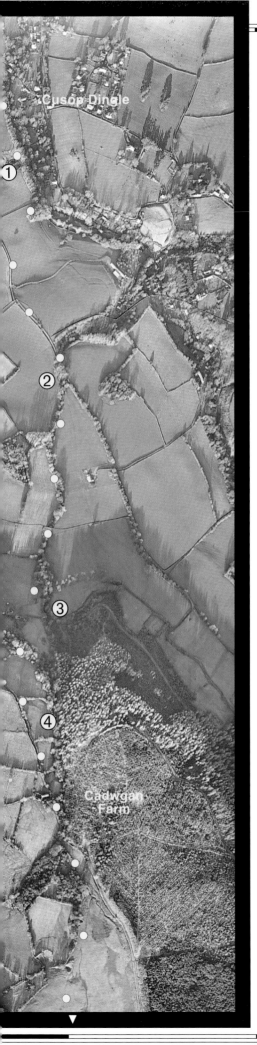

Cusop Dingle

① ② ③ ④

Cadwgan Farm

THE ROUTE FROM Hay-on-Wye to the bare uplands of the Black Mountains first leads through low-lying fields and then alongside the Dulas Brook on the edge of the lovely Cusop Dingle. Plant life here is prolific, with a riot of spring and summer flowers amidst the trees and the dense undergrowth of the stream bank. Lesser celandine, dog's mercury and primrose are the earliest flowers. The rosier hues of herb robert and campion come with the early summer though they are soon overshadowed by creamy-headed cow parsley and figwort. By late summer, foxgloves, thistles, hemp agrimony and burdock compete with the high growing grasses.

But the sylvan beauty of Cusop Dingle once harboured a metaphorical snake-in-the-grass. This was the poisoner Herbert Armstrong, a respected Hay solicitor who lived in one of the select houses amidst Cusop's leafy dells. In 1921 he was accused of attempting to poison a colleague with arsenic. The case was typical of its era. Armstrong was the archetypal domestic poisoner, fastidious and dapper, but with inner menace. The case became truly sensational when the body of Armstrong's late wife was exhumed and found to be riddled with arsenic. Katherine Armstrong's death had been diagnosed as being caused through illness but she was known to be over fond of chocolate and Armstrong was believed to have laced her regular supplies with poison. He was hanged at Gloucester and his effigy featured in Madame Tussauds' Chamber of Horrors, a long way from the sylvan peace of Cusop.

The long sweeping escarpment of Hay Bluff runs above the road to Gospel Pass

ROUTE DIRECTIONS

1. Go across the moor, keeping a wall and fencing to the right,t hen keep ahead where these boundaries veer off to the right. Go by a small disused quarry on the moorland summit and continue for ½ mile (800m) to reach a road. Hay Bluff is prominent ahead.

2. Go right along the road for a ¼ mile (400m) keeping left at a junction with a road going down right.

3. About 200yds beyond the road junction break off left on to a track by a boulder bearing the Offa's Dyke footpath sign. Follow a broad grassy track over a small stream and follow the track that rises steadily up the eastern flank of Hay Bluff. Cross a small gully with Hay Bluff rearing up to the right. Continue south-east along the track towards a small notch in the skyline ahead.

Alternative route via summit of Hay Bluff (Pen-y-Beacon) (A)

The high-level route can be reached by incorporating an ascent of Hay Bluff. This is best reached by continuing up the road from where the official Offa's Dyke Path goes off left to reach a car park after 500yds.

3a. Go left up an obvious track which zig-zags to the top of the Hay Bluff escarpment. Turn left at the lip of the escarpment and walk towards the trig point on Hay Bluff summit. From the trig point, strike due south-east along a well-worn and boggy track to the rising ground of Llech y Lladron. (See next spread.)

Alternative road route through the Vale of Ewyas (B)

In bad weather, walkers may choose to avoid the high-level route. If so, the road leading on through Gospel Pass can be followed down the Vale of Ewyas and along the banks of the Afon Honddu. It passes through Capel-y-ffin, where there is a youth hostel, and on through Llanthony to the A465 at Llanvihangel Crucorney and thence to Pandy from where the Offa's Dyke Path leads south towards Monmouth. This road route alternative is about 15 miles (24km) from the car park below Hay Bluff to Pandy.

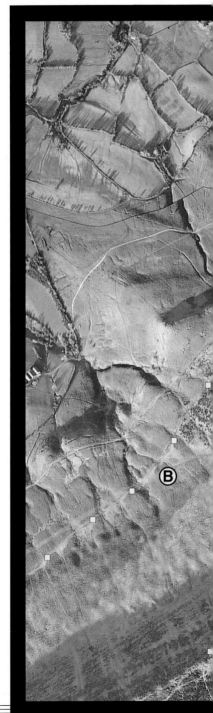

Hay Bluff to Pandy

12½ miles (20km)

This section of the path traverses the long, lonely eastern ridge of the Black Mountains. The route can be broken by a descent to the Vale of Ewyas or the Olchon valley at certain points. The path is obvious along the ridge but thick mist can be misleading. When the summits of the ridges are covered in snow, navigation can require skill and experience. Winter clothing and equipment is essential. In summer conditions, the first part of the ridge walk is across peat hags where the soft going can be tiring. The way improves later on firmer ground.

ROUTE DIRECTIONS

It is important to follow the next directions carefully, especially in misty conditions, since the linking path from this point to the Hatterrall Ridge track at Llech y Lladron is not well defined.

1. On the official route, continue up a path which leads across the tops of several steep gullies. At the top of a final gully in the sequence the path runs across some slabby rocks. There is a distinctive ditch and bank just below the path at this point.

2. To the right of the main path, two gullies run uphill. Break off right from the main path and go up the first continuation gully. Where the gully levels off at a flattish area, go ahead up a green trench that leads due south. The way soon becomes a slight but continuous path. Just beyond a rise the distinctive edge of the Hatterrall Ridge can be seen, in clear weather, lying due south. Continue along the path which soon becomes peaty and more clearly defined.

3. Pass a small pool on the right and then turn left on to the main track which leads up the slope of Llech y Lladron and on to the Hatterrall Ridge.

NOTE: The main track, which continues along the flank of the ridge from the top of the gullys (1), leads to the the Olchon valley route, a low-level alternative to the Hatterrall route in bad weather. The Olchon valley alternative can also be reached from just below the rise of Llech y Lladron where a track goes off left. This leads to the Cat's Back Ridge and to the Olchon valley. The Cat's Back Ridge is an entertaining ridge route which also requires good route-finding skills in bad weather.

4. From Llech y Lladron, continue along a well-worn route on top of the Hatterrall Ridge. The fragile peat cover has been heavily eroded by walkers who have detoured to avoid waterlogged areas. Walkers are requested whenever possible to avoid extending unnecessarily the width of the path along this peaty section.

The summit of Hay Bluff with paths radiating out

Hay Bluff

Hay Bluff

Black Hill runs roughly parallel with the path, to the east

THE WAY ALONG the Hatterrall Ridge is generally undemanding, but on this first section across the peatlands it can be heavy going underfoot in wet weather. By the end of the section the way improves as firmer ground replaces the blanket bog. There is a gentle decline from the high point of the ridge with occasional rises to lesser summits. Overall, this north-south traverse of the Hatterrall Ridge is less strenuous than its counterpart from Pandy northwards.

In driving mist the route may seem long and unrewarding, although for the true mountain lover even such harsh conditions can emphasise the sense of pleasing loneliness that such high places engender. But what distinguishes this section of the Offa's Dyke Path are the exhilarating views that can be had in clear weather from certain vantage points. Ahead lies Black Darren, with its land-slipped eastern face. Westwards across the Vale of Ewyas lie the central Black Mountains.

To the east of this section the rocky spine of the Cat's Back Ridge runs south from Black Hill and terminates in a steep bluff. The facing slope of the Cat's Back is scarred with drainage channels. Further east lie the valleys of the Monnow, the Escley Brook and the Golden valley of the River Dore.

The high ground along this section is extremely wet peat bog, typical of mountain areas and of a climate where rain is the dominant feature. Peat is not supportive of varied plant growth because of the acidity of the soil while the exposed nature of the ground and the generally low temperatures also inhibit growth. Sphagnum moss flourishes, however, and helps to build up

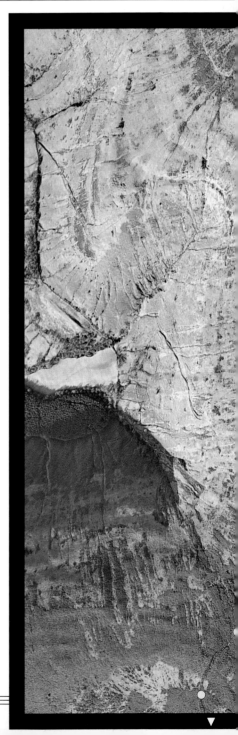

Hatterall Ridge

①

ROUTE DIRECTIONS

1. Follow the obvious track along the ridge to reach a rocky area by a painted stone. Continue along the ridge to where the ground becomes very desolate and rocky. Continue past several cairns.

the peat layer as it decays. There are 30 different types of sphagnum moss throughout the United Kingdom. Common varieties are red, yellow or green in colour. Boggy moorland supports tough mat grass and purple moor grass. Other plants which flourish here are bilberry and cotton grass.

Bird species on these Black Mountain plateaux are sparse since the infertility of the ground means it is low in nutritious plant and insect life.

1. Pass a cross-junction with paths signposted Dyffryn Olchon to the east and Capel-y-Ffin to the west, then continue to a trig point at 2,001ft (610m).
2. Continue from the trig point along an improved path over ground which becomes harder and stonier amidst grass and heather moorland. Cairns mark the way ahead.

Walkers wishing to stay at the youth hostel a mile (1.6km) north of Capel-y-Ffin can divert at (1), from the Hatterrall Ridge down the signposted path (A) into the Vale of Ewyas.

CAPEL-Y-FFIN means 'chapel on the boundary. The charming little building of St Mary's Church at Capel was built in 1762 to replace an earlier chapel. Francis Kilvert said of St Mary's, 'the whole building reminded me of an owl'. The image was typically Kilvertian. The church's squint little tower, with its louvres-like neck-feathers, certainly looks as if its head is to one side. The Baptist chapel across the river is altogether a sterner affair. It was used as a school in Victorian times.

But Capel-y-Ffin's religious connections do not end with its conventional places of worship. There was also a 'monastery' here. Named as Llanthony Monastery, the ruined outline of the building still exists. It was established by the Victorian churchman Joseph Leycester Lyne who sought to restore the monastic tradition to the Church of England. Lyne adopted the name Father Ignatius to lend credibility to his dream, part of which was the building of a monastic church to complement the monastery. But Lyne died in 1908 before his dream was realised. The community became attached to the Anglican Benedictines of Caldey Island off the Pembrokeshire coast and finally declined after the dramatic conversion of the Caldey monks to Roman Catholicism. Lyne's monastery became ruinous until acquired in 1924 by an equally powerful and eccentric figure, the sculptor Eric Gill. It later became a girls' school then had other uses, but is now privately owned.

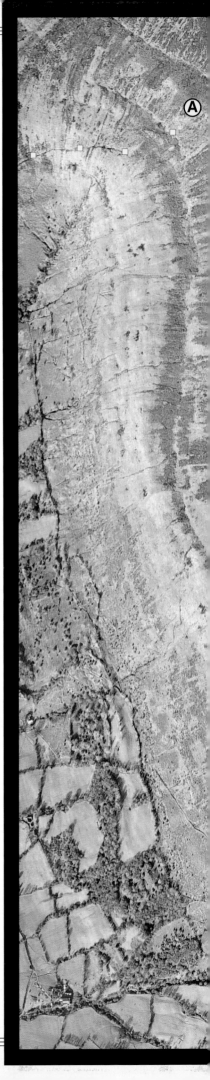

THE RIDGE ALONG this section becomes less broad-backed as it winds its way towards the summit of Hatterrall Hill. To the west, gentler slopes sweep down to Llanthony and its historic priory. The religious foundation at Llanthony is said to date from a 6th century visit by St David. Certainly Llanthony seems to have exuded an air of sanctity ever since. A hermitage was established and a church consecrated in 1108 when the warrior lord, William de Lacy, abandoned his battling with the Welsh and became an anchorite. Llanthony prospered for some years, perhaps too well since its monks became over fond of solitude and good living, although regular attacks by the Welsh must have made life miserable at times. The priory declined and was finally abandoned after the 16th century Dissolution of the monasteries.

The estate, which included Llanthony Priory, was bought in 1807 by Walter Savage Landor, the poet, playwright and essayist who was best known for his dialogues 'Imaginary Conversations'. Landor spent huge sums of money in improving the estate. The fine cedars and broad-leaved trees that survive today at Llanthony are his legacy, although plans for a mansion got no further than outbuildings. Landor had difficulty with other people. He had a track record for intransigence, having been expelled from Rugby and then Oxford. At Llanthony the poet was at odds with his neighbours, the authorities and, worst of all, his tenants. He blamed everyone in sight for his decision to leave Llanthony in 1814.

What remains of Llanthony Priory is an impressive relic of the Transitional style of Norman architecture which preceded the full glory of English Gothic and, in some ways, is more suited to the Welsh and English countryside. There is a serene but powerful atmosphere about the ruined buildings at Llanthony and the area has retained the persuasive charm which attracted its early devotees. One of the towers of the priory church and the remains of the priory lodgings have been incorporated into a modern hotel.

ROUTE DIRECTIONS

1. Reach a junction with paths going to east and west. The western path (A) descends via Loxidge Tump to Llanthony. The less definite east branch descends to the Olchon valley. Continue along the ridge.

Llanthony Priory

The lovely Vale of Ewyas and its river, the Honddu

THE VIEWS TO east and west from this narrow section of the Hatterrall Ridge reveal patterns of cultivation in stark contrast to the dark-faced hills. There is a steep fall to the east, giving sweeping views across the mouth of the Olchon valley to the Plain of Hereford. In the far distance the futuristic dishes of the Madley Satellite Earth Station can be clearly seen.

The view northwards along the Vale of Ewyas and towards the main Black Mountain range is particularly dramatic. Here the neat pattern of field boundaries in the valley bottom is emphasised by the dark pelt of trees rising towards bare upland slopes.

Walkers on this Black Mountain section of the Offa's Dyke Path can see at a glance the geographical distinctions between east and west and the dramatic contrast between England and Wales. Offa's Dyke Path threads its way along national and county boundaries, and, on its course along the Hatterrall Ridge, the route treads the modern Welsh-English border with precision.

The historical boundary work of Offa's Dyke, however, took a line much further to the east, across the Plain of Hereford, from Kington to Hereford. Yet the high ground of the Black Mountains

must have served for centuries as a natural and formidable obstacle to movements westward by colonising people. The fact that Offa's Dyke did not incorporate the great barrier of the Hatterrall Ridge in its defined line lends conviction to the belief that the Dyke may have been more territorial and administrative than defensive.

ROUTE DIRECTIONS

1. Continue along a good path from the trig point at 1,811ft (552m).
2. From a narrowing of the ridge, paths descend from the main route to the east and west. The eastern path to Longtown passes through a narrow gap and continues over some flat stones before descending more steeply into the Olchon valley. The western path begins more distinctly and trends obliquely downhill towards Llanthony which is visible below. The Offa's Dyke Path continues directly along the ridge.

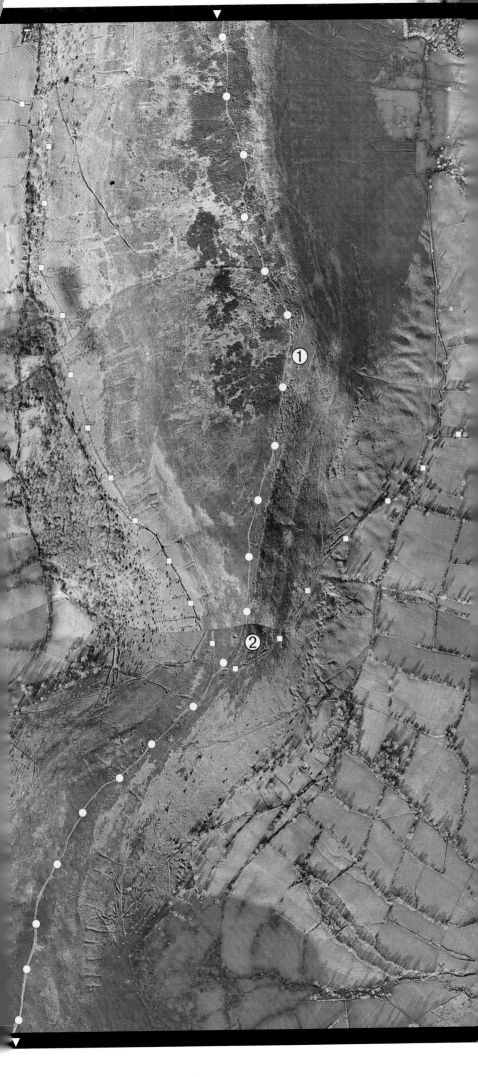

The Hatterrall Ridge is a splendid high-level stretch of the route

FROM HALFWAY ALONG this section of the path there is a good view down to the right of the land-slipped bluff of Graig above the hamlet of Cwmyoy. This landslip, like those of Black Darren, resulted from certain features of the area's underlying geological structure. At Graig, deposits of the Old Red Sandstone were separated laterally by bands of marl. After the last Ice Age, water percolated through the sandstone and lubricated the softer marl. The bands of marl were inclined towards the valley floor and the resulting 'slippery slope' caused massive downward movement of the heavy sandstone. At Graig the gap left by the movement of the sandstone from the main mass became filled with debris and is now visible as a green cultivated saddle.

The Church of St Martin at Cwmyoy is an intriguing example of the effects of this instability. Smaller incidents of land slipping have given the building a wonderfully crooked appearance, as if giant hands have tried to twist it out of shape. The tower of St Martin's leans at an alarming angle, while the body of the church flexes in the other direction. Remedial work, incorporating sturdy little supporting buttresses, adds to the illusion.

The interior of St Martin's is simple and unadorned. A rough slate floor leads up to a distorted chancel arch.

Other features are oak communion rails from the 17th century and a medieval cross.

From the Offa's Dyke Path the views to the south beyond Cwmyoy take in the low but distinctive hill of Gaer, notable as the site of Twyn y Gaer hill fort, which commanded an impressive position at 1,400ft (427m). This substantial site dates from the late Bronze-early Iron Age period, and probably began in the 5th or 4th century BC as a fenced enclosure before being extended.

To the north-west, the summit of Pen-y-Gadair Fawr, at 2,624ft (800m), stands out. It is second only in height to the nearby Waun Fach, which at 2,661ft (811m) is the highest peak of the Black Mountains. Looking northwards along the trough of the Vale of Ewyas, the summits of Rhos Dirion, 2,303ft (702m), and the Twmpa, 2,263ft (690m), can be seen at the head of the Gospel Pass.

ROUTE DIRECTIONS

1. Go uphill passing twin cairns. Just before reaching a trig point, a path leads off to the east into the Olchon valley.
2. Continue descending from the trig point over bare, stony ground.

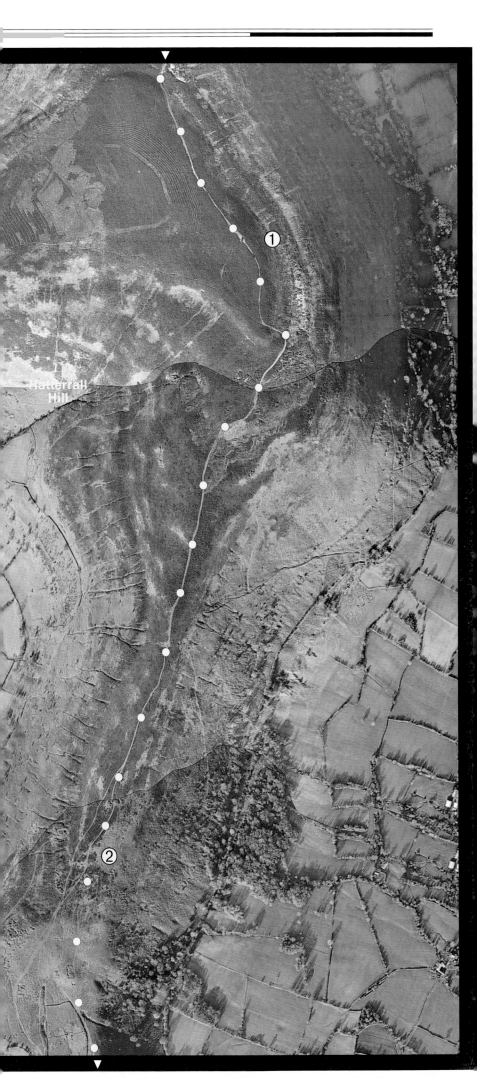

THE DESCENT FROM the Hatterrall Ridge is long and steep. South-bound walkers should feel relieved as they pass their north-bound counterparts toiling ever upwards. There is a substantial change in landscape here, from bare upland to woods and cultivated fields. One final link with the ancient frontier of the high hills comes at Pen Twyn hill fort, where the path cuts through impressive defensive embankments, dating from the pre-Roman Iron Age, similar in construction and purpose to Twyn y Gaer.

The change from hills to plain is quickly accomplished at (3), and the walker needs to navigate field path and wooded dell to reach the busy A465 at Pandy. There are a number of pubs and hotels along this stretch of the main road and there are camp sites in the Pandy area.

The village of Llanvihangel Crucorney lies ¾ mile (1.2km) south of Pandy at the southern end of the Vale of Ewyas. There is a telephone and post office here. The medieval Skirrid Inn is said to be the oldest in Wales. The handsome Tudor mansion of Llanvinhangel Court, with its 17th century additions, lies just south-east of the village.

The main town of Abergavenny lies 5 miles (8km) south of Pandy. Considered to be the 'Gateway to Wales', it is a fine market town enhanced by its surrounding hills and proud of its greatest glory, the old priory church of St Mary. There is a railway station at Abergavenny and all major services are available in the town.

ROUTE DIRECTIONS

1. Descend quite steeply, passing a walled enclosure and a farm on the right.
2. Stay on the green track as it veers to the left of a stony farm track. Go through the impressive ditch and bank ramparts of Pen Twyn hill fort. Continue past some fenced-in pine trees and descend a very steep slope, with a wall to the right, to reach a stile into a rough lane. Reach a surfaced lane and turn right up a steep rise for ¼ mile (400m) with fine open views south to the distinctive hill, The Skirrid. At a crossroads, turn left and go down the road for ¼ mile (400m).
3. Veer left and away from the lane just past a house. Go over a high stile and go diagonally left down the centre of a large field towards a straggle of trees. Continue to a lane, then turn left past Treveddw Farm to reach a T-junction.
4. Cross the road, and go down a field. Cross the railway line, and then the River Monnow by a single-file bridge. Go directly across a level field to reach the road at the Lancaster Arms, at Pandy.
5. Cross the A465, with care, then go through a gate to the right of some houses. Continue along a muddy section to a second gate and then go through a field with a fence on its right. Go over a gate with a metal step. Continue half-right to the right of a small group of trees, then continue straight ahead and up to a stile between two gates.

The Skirrid (see page 55)

Pen Twyn

PANDY

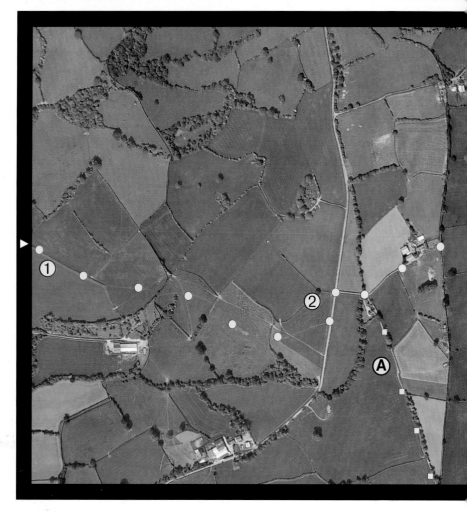

Pandy to Llantilio Crossenny

8 miles (12.8km)

The next section of the path leading south from Pandy to Llantilio Crossenny takes the walker through the quiet farming country of the Welsh Marches. On the way the route passes two fine churches, the impressive White Castle and several country inns.

Tudor Llanvihangel Court (not open)

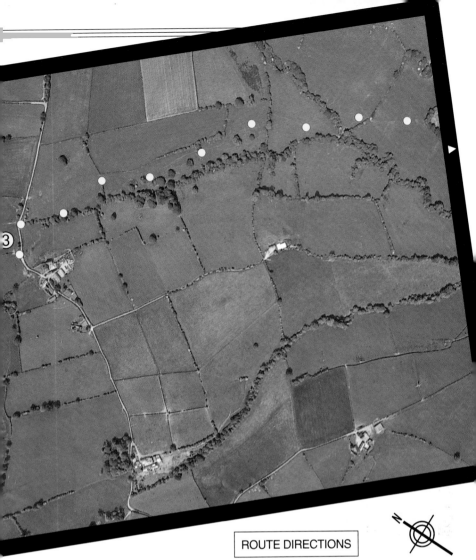

ROUTE DIRECTIONS

1. Keep the hedge to your left, then go diagonally right across the next field to stiles and a plank over a ditch. Go diagonally left across a field, just to the left of a wooded gully, and continue on to another stile and plank bridge. Continue straight ahead to stiles and a plank bridge, then keep to the highest part of the next field, before going half-left to reach a road.

2. Turn left up the road and go right at the T-junction. After 100yds turn left into the drive to Llanerch. Walk up the drive and go through a gate and down the left side of two fields to go over a stile in the left corner of the second field to a road.

3. Turn left for 100yds, then go right over a stile by a stream. Continue to a stile under a huge oak, then pass a ruined building and keep on a distinct path to a stile. Continue straight ahead over a rise.

THE COUNTRY TO the east of the A465 is rather bland in contrast with the high and wild ground of the Black Mountains. Looking back from the vicinity of Llanerch at (2), the eastern escarpment of the Hatterrall can be seen running to the north above the Olchon valley as far as the distant prow of the Cat's Back Ridge and the Black Hill.

To the south lies the distinctive sphinx-like mass of Ysgyryd Fawr, 'the big ridge'. This hill, known colloquially as The Skirrid (1,594ft/486m), has an area of landslip on its north-western shoulder, a feature caused by the same massive slippage of a sandstone mass on lubricated marl as seen at Black Darren and above Cwmyoy. Legend would have it otherwise, of course, with local stories claiming that the feature was caused by a sudden earth movement at the time of the crucifixion of Christ, or that the notch was where Noah's Ark grounded.

The Skirrid certainly has the natural style of a 'Holy Mountain' and was considered as such for many years. There are vestigial ruins of a small chapel on the summit. This chapel, probably medieval, was a place of pilgrimage until the 17th century. The main mass of The Skirrid was given to the National Trust

in 1939. The hill can be reached by keeping south for a mile (1.6km) on the lane (A) leading past the left turn into the drive to Llanerch.

This is the last of mountainous Wales for walkers on the Offa's Dyke Path. Southwards, there comes a sense of plunging into a pastoral maze of fields and spinneys, of innumerable crossings of tiny streams and sodden ditches through a fertile landscape drained by the Full Brook and the River Trothy.

The hamlet of Llangattock Lingoed with its Church of St Cadog

THE SMALL HAMLET of Llangattock Lingoed is a charming place. There is a pleasant inn, the Hunter's Moon, which lies a short distance down the road from the church. (There is a telephone box near the inn.) Llangattock is one of those quiet, relatively anonymous settlements but with an enduring sense of community in spite of rural depopulation. At its heart lies the Church of St Cadog which takes

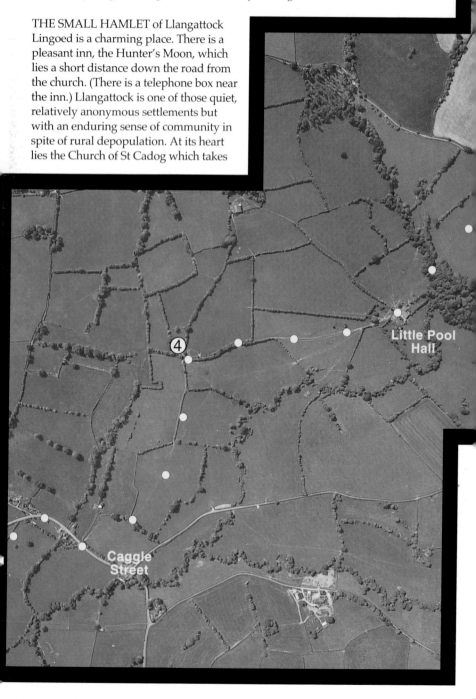

Little Pool Hall

④

Caggle Street

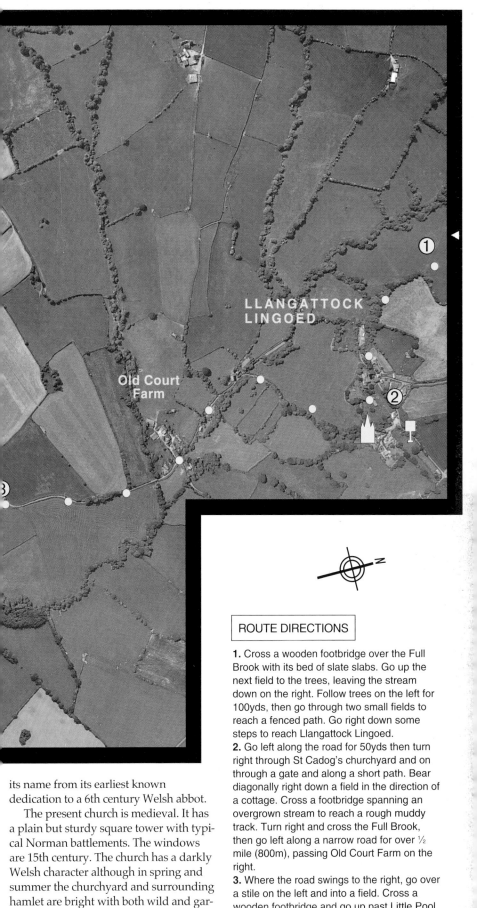

its name from its earliest known dedication to a 6th century Welsh abbot.

The present church is medieval. It has a plain but sturdy square tower with typical Norman battlements. The windows are 15th century. The church has a darkly Welsh character although in spring and summer the churchyard and surrounding hamlet are bright with both wild and garden flowers. The interior of St Cadog's is equally dark and simple. A splendid feature is the surviving breast summer, or bres summer, the upper beam of the 15th century rood screen, which now spans the entrance to the chancel.

ROUTE DIRECTIONS

1. Cross a wooden footbridge over the Full Brook with its bed of slate slabs. Go up the next field to the trees, leaving the stream down on the right. Follow trees on the left for 100yds, then go through two small fields to reach a fenced path. Go right down some steps to reach Llangattock Lingoed.

2. Go left along the road for 50yds then turn right through St Cadog's churchyard and on through a gate and along a short path. Bear diagonally right down a field in the direction of a cottage. Cross a footbridge spanning an overgrown stream to reach a rough muddy track. Turn right and cross the Full Brook, then go left along a narrow road for over ½ mile (800m), passing Old Court Farm on the right.

3. Where the road swings to the right, go over a stile on the left and into a field. Cross a wooden footbridge and go up past Little Pool Hall and continue along a track.

4. Pass a large barn on the right, then go left over a stile. Continue over a rise with a fine view of White Castle a mile (1.6km) to the south-east. Bear right down a field to reach the B4521 at Caggle Street.

White Castle

③

GREAT
TREADAM

1. Turn right and go along the B4521 for about 200yds, then go over a stile on the right and cross two fields. Swing left to a metal bridge supported on stone-filled cages across the River Trothy, or Troddu. Continue steeply uphill through several fields linked by stiles.
2. Pass Duke's Barn, then go left and up the left side of a field to gain a track, which swings round to the left of White Castle to emerge at the entrance gateway. The castle is well worth a visit.

3. Go right down the road from White Castle to pass White Castle cottages on the right. Just past a large farmhouse on the right, take the rough track branching off right. After ¾ mile (1.2km) go left at the road and then after 100yds go left again up the drive to Great Treadam. Where the drive swings left before buildings, go across a track and then through a gate on the right.

THE DOMINANT FEATURE on this section of the path is the impressive ruin of the moated White Castle. This was the most strategic of three Norman castles within an area known as the Welsh Trilateral, the others being Grosmont, 6 miles (9.6km) to the north and Skenfrith, 7 miles (11.2km) to the east. There is a waymarked 'Three Castles Walk' of about 18 miles (28.8km) linking White Castle, Grosmont and Skenfrith by an enjoyable circular route.

The three strongholds are believed to have been built by William Fitz Osbern, a leading supporter of William the Conqueror. Fitz Osbern was rewarded for his part in the Battle of Hastings by being made Earl of Hereford. With typical Norman thoroughness, he established control of the valley of the River Monnow and the main routes from England into Wales by building motte and bailey fortifications at the three sites.

White Castle would probably have been built initially as an earth mound crowned with a timber tower and with a court or palisaded bailey extending in front of it. The castle was added to substantially in the 12th and 13th century. By 1400 White Castle would have had the building outline of what is seen today. The deep moat with its stone revetment was probably a dry defence, but was no less formidable because of it.

The castle was known originally as Castell Gwyn, possibly after a previous Welsh commander of the pre-Norman district. Its present name is said to derive from the white rendering which covered its walls in the 13th century. This may explain the source of Castell Gwyn as being from the Welsh gwyn for white. Such distinctive rendering would have served as weathering and as a visual expression of the castle as a powerful military stronghold on the frontier between Wales and England.

White Castle prospered throughout the medieval period under different lordships as kings and subjects quarrelled. Its greatest military use came in the mid-13th century during the civil war between Henry III and Simon de Montfort and at a time when the Welsh ruler, Llywelyn ap Gruffyd, took up arms against Henry. It was at this time that the formidable D-shaped towers were added. After the conquest of Wales by Edward I, White Castle was retained as an administrative centre. But by the 16th century the castle was derelict, an indication that the great struggle for Welsh Wales had ended.

White Castle, one of the three known as the Welsh Trilateral

Hen Gwrt

① ②

1. Keep left along a field to reach a stile. Bear diagonally left down the next field keeping in line with the spire of St Teilo's Church which can be seen rising from trees at Llantilio Crosseny. Cross more fields, bearing slightly right across a final field to reach the B4233. (A short distance along the road to the left lies the medieval moated site of Hen Gwrt, the 'Old Court' of the ecclesiastical see of the Bishop of Llandaff.)

2. Cross the road, go through a kissing-gate and then cross two fields to reach the road at Llantilio Crossenny. (The Hostry Inn is a short distance up to the right.)

3. Turn left and go down the road for a short distance. (St Teilo's Church is about 200yds further on.) Just over a bridge, go right through a kissing-gate, and shortly, cross a stream via a single-file footbridge. Turn left and reach the road. Keep left along the road. (This point can be reached directly along the road which leads south-east from the Hostry Inn.)

St Teilo's Church at Llantilio Crossenny

Llantilio Crossenny to Monmouth

9 miles (14.4km)

The route to Monmouth from Llantilio Crossenny continues its meandering course through a quiet countryside of fields and woods and farmsteads. The way crosses the valley of the River Trothy and then rises over the darkly wooded King's Wood Hill before descending to the historic town of Monmouth.

THE WALKER IS guided towards Llantilio Crossenny by the shapely spire of St Teilo's Church, a symbol of the area's rich tradition and substantial history. Such history is in evidence at the site of Hen Gwrt a short distance west of the church and close to the Offa's Dyke Path.

All that remains of this medieval site is its moated enclosure as the stonework of Hen Gwrt was pillaged by a local landowner for use in the building of Llantilio Court during the late 18th century. The Court itself is now a vestigial ruin just north of the church. Hen Gwrt dates from the 14th century and was the administrative centre of a large ecclesiastical estate belonging to the Bishop of Llandaff. This manor later became a deer park under the ownership of the Herberts of Raglan Castle. Hen Gwrt became the hunting lodge.

Llantilio Crossenny's early

prominence dates from the 6th century when a local chieftain called Ynyr, or Iddon, was said to be under threat from pagan Saxons. Ynyr appealed to Teilo, the Bishop of Llandaff, who responded with prayers. The Saxons were defeated in battle and Teilo received a grant of land from the grateful Ynyr who had fought under the standard of a large wooden cross at the site of the present church.

The present church is particularly pleasing. It is mainly 12th and 13th century, with some major changes from the 14th century. St Teilo's shingled spire is an elegant addition of the 18th century. The central tower is supported internally by four massive arches. The 60ft (20m) trunks of four trees support the bells within the tower and the tower space creates a delightful grotto-like effect where it leads through to the chancel with its intricate stonework.

THE AREA OF THE River Trothy through which the path now leads lies at the very heart of the Welsh Marches. It is a land of quiet farms and narrow lanes fringed by tall hedgerows, representing the very best of border farming country with stock grazing on the well-grassed and well-watered fields.

Historically, this was a countryside which was in dispute from earliest times. The line of Offa's Dyke lies over 20 miles (32km) to the north and east but Saxon interest would have extended into the area if only through territorial imperative. The land would not have been particularly manageable during the Dark Ages since it was likely to have been thickly wooded and would have had few lines of communication. By Norman times things had changed, however, and the Norman and medieval presence so evident at Llantilio Crossenny and elsewhere indicates a growing interest by the conquerors in what promised to be a rich agricultural countryside of great strategic value.

The remains of a motte and bailey south of where the path leaves the road

below Penrhos Farm suggests that Norman fortifications other than the Three Castles were established in this strategic area. This smaller relic may have been erected by a lesser figure than Fitz Osbern of White Castle, but its structure is of the same design as the original White Castle. This is a particularly well preserved feature which was once lightly wooded but is now clear of trees.

Such structures were the first Norman strongholds to be built and were quickly raised by the use of unskilled labour. The motte was a high mound of earth on top of which was placed a timber tower as the ultimate defence work. A ditch was excavated round the larger bailey with earth being banked up on the inner perimeter and a wooden palisade established. In later years motte and bailey construction was superseded by stone built castles like White, Grosmont and Skenfrith. But the one described here may have quickly fallen out of use.

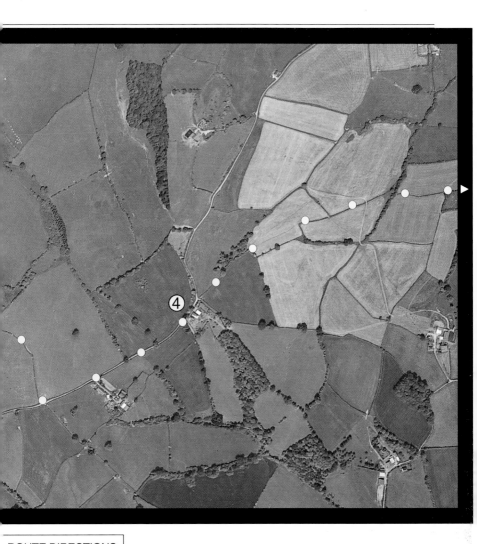

ROUTE DIRECTIONS

1. Continue along the road to pass Penrhos Farm.

2. Leave the road by going left over a stile. Continue up a field, then descend to cross a plank bridge and a stile. Go left and over a stile by a ruined building. Continue towards Grange Farm ahead.

3. Cross the house drive and go through a narrow gate with a house on the left. Please keep close to the fence of the horse schooling ring on the right. Go over a stile and continue down afield keeping close to the left-hand hedge as it curves round to the right to reach a road. Turn left and go along the road for ⅓ mile (500m).

4. Where the road bends to the left just by a house, go over a stile on the right. Continue down a field with a hedge to the left.

The clear evidence of a motte and bailey, near Penrhos Farm

Not much remains of Grace Dieu Abbey, onetime sister house of Tintern

THE PATH ON THIS section goes through attractive countryside, following the River Trothy for part of the way. Where the path leaves the road at Pen-pwll-y-calch, it follows a typical field hedge. Such hedges can be ancient and are fruitful habitats for all manner of flora and fauna. Blackthorn binds the base of the hedge and bramble overruns it. Hedgerows are a fast diminishing feature in some parts of Britain and are now protected by law.

Blackthorn is a common hedgerow shrub, its white flowers emerging between March and May before the leaves uncurl. The fruit of the blackthorn is the bitter sloe. Other hedgerow shrubs are hawthorn, elder, dogwood, maple and wild privet, all of which are common along the length of the Offa's Dyke Path.

Here in the valley of the Trothy the patchwork fields, divided by broad hedgerows, merge with stands of woodland. The path leads pleasantly towards the quiet little Church of St Michael and All Angels at Llanvihangel-Ystern-Llewern. This is a delightful church which walkers treat with affection and respect. It has an attractive pyramidal cap spire and simple features.

ROUTE DIRECTIONS

1. Go over a stile and follow an obvious path down across the field. The Church of St Michael and All Angels can be seen amidst trees ahead. Go down to a stream and a stile-bridge, then ascend to cross a lane head.
2. Cross a small meadow where the path may be overgrown. Cross a footbridge over the small stream and continue with the church on your right to reach a road. (The church can be visited by diverting from the path through a gate into the churchyard or by continuing to the road and entering through a dark stand of coppiced beech trees.)

3. On reaching the road by the church, turn right, then left through a gate to continue for 200yds along a drive to Sunnybank. The River Trothy is down to your left.
4. Reach a metal field-gate on the left. Continue past the gate for a few yards, then go sharp left over a hidden stile in the hedge. Turn right along the field edge and continue through fields. The path can be very muddy here. Bear right along the base of a small rounded hill where the path comes close to the river.
5. Cross the line of a ditch by a bend in the river, then bear right and over the side of a small hill to continue via fields and stiles towards a road.

N

⑤

FIELD PATHS and quiet lanes lead up to the tree-shaded heights of King's Wood on this section of the path. But first the way leads across the River Trothy and on past the site of the 13th-century Grace Dieu Abbey. Nothing survives of this Cistercian monastery which was a sister house to the great abbey at Tintern.

The Cistercian order, founded by Benedictine monks in Citeaux, France, was noted for solitude and poverty and its monasteries were established in

remote and quiet places. Tintern has become a major tourist attraction in the now less than remote Wye valley. But Grace Dieu seems to have suffered the same fate as other monastic houses when Henry VIII's Dissolution orders led to them being pillaged for building stone.

Hendre Farm was the home of the Llangattock family whose most famous son was Charles Stewart Rolls of the Rolls-Royce partnership. Rolls was a remarkably gifted inventor who combined his talents with the engineering genius of Royce and also supplied financial backing for their ventures. Rolls was also adventurous. He pioneered advances in aviation, motoring and ballooning until his tragic death in a flying accident in 1910. He also experimented with early aerial photography. Rolls is commemorated at the heart of Monmouth where there is a bronze sculpture of him in Agincourt Square.

The way leads through the attractive King's Wood where a mix of deciduous and conifer trees creates a mature woodland area that is now managed. The mix includes yew trees, which were the favourite source of the supple longbows said to have enabled Welsh archers to draw the bowstring to the ear with devastating effect, not least at Crecy and Agincourt.

ROUTE DIRECTIONS

1. Turn left along the road for 300yds, crossing the River Trothy via Abbey Bridge.
2. Leave the road by going right just before a house, then go over a stile. Keep alongside the hedge on the left, go over a stile and bear left past some scrubby ground which is the site of Grace Dieu Abbey. Cross a single file bridge at some elder trees.
3. Cross the middle of a long field, then go over a stile and on to a solitary oak tree. Go sharp right over a stile by the oak tree and turn left down the field edge. Cross a footbridge and continue up to a a stile on to a road by a house.
4. Go right for ¼ mile (400m) along the road, passing Hendre Farm on the way. At Lower Hendre the road bends sharply left and uphill.
5. Where the road bends sharply to the right keep straight on off the road and along a rough track which merges with a stony track leading up into the trees of King's Wood.
6. Keep ahead at a crossing of forestry tracks and follow a muddy rutted track through the trees and over the brow of a hill. Where the forestry track bends sharply to the right, continue straight ahead and down through trees on narrower track.

King's Wood

ROUTE DIRECTIONS

1. Follow the tree-shrouded track downhill, passing, on the left, a parish boundary stone dated 1857. The western face of the stone seems to have been defaced. The track is very muddy and rutted here. A short distance beyond the boundary stone, take the right-hand fork in the path.

2. Cross a forestry road, then continue downhill on a track which soon branches down to the right. This section can be very muddy and slippery.

3. Go over a footbridge then bear right to emerge into a field. Follow the path along the bottom edge of the field beside trees.

4. Go right through trees and across an attractive single-file footbridge. Continue up a wooded slope, then turn left along the field edge with a deep ditch down left.

5. Cross a footbridge over a ditch and continue along the edge of a field to reach Watery Lane. Turn left and follow Watery Lane for about ¾ mile (1.2km) to reach the B4233.

Monmouth, sandwiched between the Monnow and the Wye. Agincourt Square at the centre of the town (left) is dominated by Shire Hall

Monmouth to Brockweir

10 miles (16km)

1. Turn right on to the B4233 and continue along Drybridge Street. Turn left at a roundabout and cross Monnow Bridge through the famous 13th century gatehouse. Continue up Monnow Street to reach Agincourt Square.

2. Continue past the 18th century Shire Hall, and where the road bears left keep right along the pedestrianised Church Street. Where Church Street merges with Whitecross Street, by St Mary's Church, turn sharp right down St Mary's Street.

3. Turn left into St James Street, then go immediately right down Wye-bridge Street. Cross left, with care, and cross the very busy A40 via a pedestrian subway. Cross Wye Bridge and keep straight ahead past where the A466 branches right. Continue along the A4136 and where the road swings left and uphill by the Mayhill Hotel, cross to the other side.

4. Go right up a path bordered by railings where it rises through trees above the road. Go through a kissing-gate and continue along a field to where another kissing-gate leads out on to a road. Follow the road steeply uphill for ¼ mile (400m).

5. Where the road bends sharply right by the entrance to a service reservoir go ahead off the road, sign-posted Beaulieu Wood, and bear left through a kissing-gate and on to a tree-shaded path. Climb steadily along a slightly overgrown path. Where the path levels off, bear right over a stile and follow the path through afield bearing slightly up left towards some houses. There are magnificent views from here across Monmouth and towards the Welsh Hills.

6. Reach a surfaced lane, then go up left for a few yards past a house on the right to go over a stile on the left into a shady conifer plantation. Climb steeply, then bear down right into a worn gully and continue uphill over twisted tree routes and rocks. Reach a distinctive rocky barrier with tree trunks embedded in it. Go right up some rock steps, then bear up left to the summit of The Kymin.

Go right towards the Round House, keeping to its left and continue down a drive. (A detour to the right of the Round House gives magnificent views to the west and leads to the intriguing Naval Temple.) Go left through a kissing-gate, just past the car park, and follow a path. Go through another kissing-gate and continue through fields.

THE REDBROOK AREA takes up the central part of this section and presents a fascinating contrast to the park-like style of The Kymin. Yet there seems little change in the rural nature of the countryside as the path leads steadily downhill from The Kymin to reach the road at Upper Redbrook. But this is an industrial area famed for its iron works. Its position in a valley where water was in good supply and easily harnassed made Redbrook the ideal site for processing the rich haematite found in the Forest of Dean. Iron-working was carried out here from medieval times although there was probably smelting at Redbrook in Roman times, and some kind of metal-working before that. Furnaces were well established by the 17th century and Redbrook flourished for many years.

Throughout the 18th and 19th centuries the valley of Upper Redbrook and the banks of the Wye at Lower Redbrook bustled with industry as foundries and mills and forges processed metals, including copper imported from Cornwall. The name Redbrook may have arisen from the iron-oxide colour of the streams that were harnessed through millponds and wheels. There was a tinplate company at Redbrook until 1961 when modern strip mills elsewhere finally brought an end to a remarkable industrial tradition at the heart of the countryside.

A short distance east of Redbrook is the village of Newland, distinguished by the splendid Church of All Saints which boasts a rather stately setting. Newland church is known as the 'Cathedral of the Forest'. Its relative grandeur reflects the mineral wealth of the Forest of Dean. The source of that wealth is symbolised by a famous bas-relief 'miners brass' depicting a 14th century miner. Alongside the church there is a row of fine old almshouses, now modernised but dating from the early 17th century. Newland also has a delightfully named inn, the Ostrich.

ROUTE DIRECTIONS

1. Go through fields and over stiles. Continue round the edge of some rough ground down on the right, then continue over stiles to reach a path which leads left, past a building, and on to a rough lane.

2. Continue down the lane passing Duffield Farm on the left. The lane becomes very steep. Just beyond a sharp right-hand bend, at Sunnybank Cottage, the lane becomes surfaced and leads down to the road at Upper Redbrook.

3. Turn right and go down the road for ¼ mile (400m), watching for traffic. Cross over just before the point where an incline bridge spans the road. Go left along a lane, which leads out of Wales and into England, between houses and on to the A466 at Lower Redbrook. There is a café/restaurant on the opposite side of the road.

4. Go left along the A466 past St Saviour's Church, a telephone kiosk, post office and shop. Continue for 100yds then turn left before the Bell Inn. Go up 67 comfortably spaced steps. Cross a narrow road and go up a steep lane. The view north along the Wye valley is impressive from here. About 50yds up the steep lane bear left up some steps and over a stile. Climb a steep grassy path.

5. Continue over two stiles to a T-junction with a track at Highbury Farm. Go right and follow the track up and round to the left.

The Naval Temple, built by a local gentlemen's club in 1800 on The Kymin

73

Highbury
Wood

A466

Coxbury
Farm

① ② ③

THERE IS A certain pleasure for the walker in being reunited with Offa's Dyke in the wooded depths of Highbury. The Dyke was last seen on Rushock Hill, 55 miles (88km) to the north. From Rushock Hill its line runs across the Plain of Hereford through Hereford town and on to the south via English Bicknor.

There are few traces of the Dyke, however, until its emphatic presence in Highbury Wood, 450ft (136m) above the Wye. Here the Dyke reaches a maximum height of 76ft (23m) including its eastern spoil trench. The natural steepness of the western slope towards the Wye makes the earthwork truly formidable. Cyril Fox charted the line of the Dyke through Highbury Woods during 1931. He did this with great difficulty due to the overgrown nature of the ground. 'This was the first time that movement along the line of the Dyke was found to be physically impossible without the use of a billhook', reported Fox.

Highbury Plains, as its name implies, would have been clear ground in Offa's time – as indicated by the accuracy and proportions of the Dyke. Highbury was farmed as late as last century but reverted to a broad-leaved woodland of yew, oak, beech, ash, lime, wild service tree and hazel. The path through Highbury makes for delightful walking, with woodland to the left and the steep fall of wooded slopes to the right.

Fallow deer frequent these woodlands, as do the tiny muntjac deer, although the latter are unlikely to be seen by the walker. Fallow deer were native to Britain thousands of years ago but the species died out after the last Ice Age. They were reintroduced by the Normans. In the Wye valley area fallow deer can vary in colour. The most common colouring is a coat with a reddish upper part with white speckling and pale cream under parts, although a black or dark brown upper coat is also common. Fallow deer are shy, secretive creatures. The best chance of seeing them is in the early morning, or at dusk. A sighting, however fleeting, is always exhilarating.

ROUTE DIRECTIONS

1. Where the track reaches a gate, go over a stile on the right and into Highbury Wood. This fine area of broad-leaved woodland is a National Nature Reserve. (Because of important conservation needs, anyone wishing to divert from the footpath should apply for a permit from English Nature.) After about 100yds the path merges with the line of Offa's Dyke and runs along a high section of the earthwork.
2. The path swings right and downhill in line with a sketchy section of the Dyke on the right. Go over a stile, cross a muddy lane and go through a gate. Continue downhill with the broad bank of the Dyke on your left to go over a stile by a gnarled old tree. Turn left and continue along the top of the Dyke, then go along an open field with the Dyke on the left.
3. Pass Coxbury Farm on the left. Continue alongside a uniform section of grassed-over Dyke.

Newland with its stately church

75

Bigsweir House, downstream of Bigsweir Bridge

BEYOND COXBURY FARM the path leads through two contrasting areas of woodland. The first is a small conifer plantation with a significant lack of plant life on the woodland floor, typical of the rather barren nature of such plantations. Here sunlight fails to penetrate and there is little richness in the leaf mould. Beyond the conifers, the path leads below rising slopes towards the broad-leaved acres of Creeping Hill Wood. Offa's Dyke is to the right of this field section but is not discernible, possibly because the steepness of the cultivated ground to the left would cause earth to 'drift' downhill and merge with the Dyke.

Creeping Hill is a broad-leaved wood on the slopes of Wyegate Hill. Open and sun-dappled compared with conifer plantations, here the understorey is rich and fruitful and supports a variety of woodland flowers. In springtime, drifts of bluebells are a particular delight.

Offa's Dyke takes a definite uphill course on Wyegate Hill to a height of 550ft (167m) and then descends quite steeply once more. Fox suggests that the reason for this sharp alignment was the Mercian's desire to 'maintain wherever possible a commanding alignment above the Wye'.

The path leads down through Creeping Hill Wood to reach the road above Bigsweir Bridge and the A466. A diversion from the Offa's Dyke Path can be made to St Briavels from here (A) for walkers who may wish to stay at the delightful St Briavels Castle youth hostel. The walk to St Briavels is quite steep as the village stands on a commanding position 650ft (198m) above the Wye. A meander of the river once ran below the steep ground on which St Briavels now stands. This was a similar feature to an ancient meander at Redbrook and Newland. Both meanders became cut off as the parent river sliced more deeply into the present gorge.

St Briavels is a village of great charm. The Norman castle was once the administrative and judicial centre of the Forest of Dean. Its surviving gate house and towers and restored walls are impressive, and its modern use as a youth hostel offers a special kind of hospitality. The area round the once moated castle has been imaginatively restored by the local Moat Society of St Briavels. The Church of St Mary the Virgin stands opposite the castle and has some fine features. The village lies comfortably alongside the castle and has a pub, shops, post office and telephone.

ROUTE DIRECTIONS

1. Go over a stile into a dark conifer plantation, then on through fields and over stiles with high ground to the left and trees to the right.

2. Go into Creeping Hill Wood and follow the path uphill on the Dyke, then soon bear down right on a path leading away from where the Dyke veers uphill. Continue downhill, crossing the line of the Dyke once more, to reach a stile into a lane by a house.

3. Turn right down the lane to reach a road. There is a telephone box about 20yds up the road to the left. Turn right down the road. (Immediately on the left is the start of a path (A) which leads in 1½ miles (2.4km) to St Briavels youth hostel.)

4. Go left on reaching the A466. See page 78 for a choice of alternative routes from this point.

A466

① ② ③ ④ Ⓐ

Creeping
Hill

Bigsweir
Bridge

There is a choice of routes from Bigsweir to Brockweir. One leads inland and although complex and very steep in places, is interesting nonetheless. The alternative route follows the east bank of the River Wye. It is undemanding and makes a pleasant change from the rise and fall of inland walking.

Inland Route

1. Bear left from the junction with the A446, then go left through a gate by the lodge of St Briavels House. Shortly take a right fork beneath some mature oaks. Go over a cattle grid, then continue diagonally left across a field, climbing towards the far corner. Go over a stile to the right of a gate in the wall, then continue forward and slightly to the right up the next field to a wooden signpost.

2. Go over a stile into woods. In 25yds keep left and climb very steeply through a mix of beech, sycamore, ash, oak and hazel. Near the top of this section, go up some ridged planks with a useful handrail then go up two stone steps and turn right at a T-junction. On reaching a stone wall, turn left up an enclosed path with the wall to the right. The climb eases here. Reach a road opposite the gates of Birchfield House.

3. Turn right along the road, bearing left at Sittingreen. Ascend gently then take the first lane on the right (no through road sign). Follow the unsurfaced lane past a house on the right. Where the track bears right by a field gate, go left beneath an oak tree on an enclosed stony path which becomes a track leading gently uphill to a road.

4. Turn right at the road. After 150yds pass Denehurst and 50yds further on go left over a stile into a field. Continue forward with a barn on the left to go over two stiles. Cross a grassy area to the left of some sycamores, then ascend with a house on the right and reach a stile and metal gate by a shed in the top right-hand corner of a meadow.

5. Go left along an unsurfaced farm lane and just past an old stone stile turn right down an enclosed path. After 100yds, take the right fork in the path and descend through trees. DO NOT go over the waymarked stile on the left. (This is not the Offa's Dyke Path.) Continue past houses and come out on to the end of a metalled road. Continue to a T-junction with another road and turn left.

River Route

1a. Bear left at the junction with the A446 and continue past the gate by the lodge of St Briavels Hall. Go left over a stile just before the traffic lights at Bigsweir Bridge. Follow the river bank. Cross a sturdy wooden footbridge over a small stream and continue along the river bank to a stile.

2a. Go over the stile on to the drive of St Briavels Hall. Turn right and go along the drive with the river on your right and lovely mixed woodland up on the left. There is an abundance of fern varieties here. Where the drive curves slightly to the left up to tall concrete gate posts, bear right on to a path which leads among trees along the river's edge.

3a. Keep right where the path divides. Go over a stile to the right of a metal gate into a field, then follow the curve of the river. Llandogo village can be seen on the opposite bank.

4a. Go over a stile in a fence on the left of a wooden gate and continue through a field next to the river. At the end of this section, where the path narrows beneath the trees, the ground may become muddy where cattle have congregated.

5a. Go through a wooden gate and along a path in the woods, then go through a metal gate and follow the river bank through a long meadow. The river runs through a stretch of rapids here.

1A

1

2A

2

3

4

5

St Briavels
Common

1A

1

2A

A466

BROCKWEIR

3A

Ⓐ

★ Tintern
Abbey

Brockweir to Sedbury Cliff

8 miles (12.8km)

This final section of Offa's Dyke continues high above the River Wye where Dyke and path merge amidst lovely woods. The going can be strenuous in places but the exhilarating views from the cliffs of the Lower Wye, and the sense of final achievement, spur the walker on to Sedbury.

ROUTE DIRECTIONS

Inland route continued

1. Continue down the road past several houses. Where the road bends sharply left, turn right down an enclosed path. Cross a narrow lane and continue down a path, to the left of a house called Shangri-La, to reach a road.

2. Go left along the road, then go immediately right down the drive to Brook House. At the gate to Brook House take the path down to the right, cross a stream then go right and up to a rough road. Continue ahead to a road. The Mackenzie Hall lies up to the left. (Brockweir village, with shops, inn, post office, telephone, and access to the A466 is a five-minute walk downhill to the right. A linking path to the main Offa's Dyke Path can be gained from Brockweir. See below.)

3. Cross the road diagonally right and follow a path into woodland. Go over a stile and down left on a broad muddy track, then bear down right and across a stream. Follow a faint path up a very steep slope to reach a large wooden signpost where the route from Brockweir comes in from the right. Bear up left along a broad track into trees.

4. At a gate, go over a stile into a field and turn right alongside a wire fence. After 50yds go sharp left and climb steeply up the field on vestigial Dyke. At top of the field bear left, then up right on a rocky path to reach the top of a bank. Go along the bank to a stile on to the start of a particularly fine section of Offa's Dyke. This first part can be very muddy. Cross a farm track and continue up steep wooden steps bedded with gravel. The Dyke is on your right. Continue pleasantly along the crest of the Dyke through the woods.

5. Path and Dyke swing round to the left. Continue, passing a path (A) to Tintern (1 mile/1.6km) going down right.

River route continued

1a. Continue past a boathouse and over a stile. Keep to the river's edge through a long field.

2a. Go over another stile and follow a riverside path to reach a road which is followed to Brockweir.

3a. From the quayside, go up to the village and turn right just past the Brockweir Country Inn, then turn right down a surfaced lane past the stables of the Horse and Pony Protection Association. (Friendly residents in fields and yard.) Go sharp left just past the stables at a signpost to Devil's Pulpit. Continue steadily uphill to reach a large wooden signpost at the junction with the main Offa's Dyke Path. Bear ahead and to the right along a broad track into trees. Follow on from (4) above.

TINTERN WAS A Cistercian foundation of 1131 which thrived until the Dissolution of the monasteries in 1536. Although subsequently robbed of stone for building purposes, the present-day ruins are impressive and a popular tourist draw.

The monks established a tradition of metal working at the abbey and during the mid-16th century, long after the monks were gone, a wire-work industry developed around the abbey ruins and was to flourish for over 200 years.

Famous Tintern Abbey, a tourist attraction since the 18th century

It was the Romantic Movement which saw the start of Tintern's tourism era. The 'sublime' experience of rediscovered Gothic architecture and the appeal of the picturesque made Tintern and the Wye valley major attractions. The abbey was visited by Wordsworth and J. M. W. Turner, among many other literary and artistic figures. Wealthy sight-seers soon followed as foreign holidays became less attractive because of the Napoleonic Wars. Today Tintern Abbey has been stripped of much of its ivy and its 'picturesque' charm, while its crumbling walls have been efficiently pre-served. The result has meant a loss of the Romantic image of Wordsworth and Turner's day, but the ruin is still inspiring.

ROUTE DIRECTIONS

N

1. Go up wooden steps and turn right, ignoring a stile into field. Continue to Devil's Pulpit, with its splendid views down to Tintern Abbey. Continue along the top of the Dyke on a stony path and over awkward tree roots to pass a memorial seat.
2. Continue into Worgan's Wood. Subsidiary paths can be confusing here for a short distance, but keep to the main path. Keep left when a path to Tintern via the old Wye Valley Railway line goes off right. The path can be muddy and rough underfoot here. At across path through the Dyke, go down right, then left, and continue with a forestry road down to the right.
3. Go through a gap in the wall on the left and continue with Dyke and crowning wall on the right. Cross a forestry road, and continue past massive beech trees. The path can be muddy here.
4. Go down steps and cross a stony track. Climb steeply up a stepped path in the dark shade of trees. Continue with a wire fence on the left to reach a sharp left turn over a stile. Follow a path, fenced to either side, to reach the B4228.

Tintern Abbey can be reached down the path mentioned on the previous path at (5). It can also be reached by the path at (2) on this spread. The return trip to Offa's Dyke involves a a stiff climb in both cases.

ROUTE DIRECTIONS

1. Turn right down the B4228 for ⅓ mile (500m), then go left over a stile opposite the drive to Boughcliffe. There are marvellous views of the Severn Bridge ahead. Go over two more stiles and on through fields.

2. Enter a wood via a stile by a big ash tree. Turn sharply left after 150yds and continue along a narrow path with a wire fence and an open field on the left. Swing right to go alongside a driveway on the left. Go down the left side of a meadow to reach the B4228 once more.

3. Go left down the road for about ⅓ mile (500m). Cross the road just before a group of houses is reached at Woodcroft. A dramatic viewpoint over the River Wye lies just to the right. Go off to the right from the road along a path directly above Wintour's Leap.

4. Pass a deep quarry down on the right and continue past the quarry entrance to cross a bend in a rough road, (the Rising Sun pub is down to the left). Continue straight ahead on to a shaded path.

5. Go through two kissing-gates and on down a path to reach an archway on to a main road. Turn right along the road for 50yds. Go right through a kissing-gate and follow a path to where it bends right. Go sharp left over a stile and straight across a field to a stile. Turn right, then left along a passageway.

6. Turn right down a field and go over a stile, bearing left. Continue across a field keeping to the right of the distinctive Twtshill Tower to reach a road. Chepstow Castle can be seen ahead.

THERE IS NOT much evidence of Offa's Dyke in the immediate vicinity of this stretch of the path. The main feature of the area is the distinctive Lancaut Peninsula which can be seen from the viewpoint above Wintour's Leap. The remains of an impressive promontory fort dating from the Iron Age occupy the neck of the Lancaut Peninsula. Fox suggested that part of the eastern embankment of the fort was incorporated by Offa into his 8th century earthwork.

Wintour's Leap gained its name from the Royalist Sir John Wintour who was reputed to have leapt astride his horse into the river below, to escape successfully from Parliamentarian pursuers. The cliff is 200ft (60m) sheer at this point and Sir John's famous leap is either apocryphal or took place at a less spectacular point.

From (3) onwards, the Offa's Dyke Path leads through increasingly built-up areas, but is still of interest. Impressive limestone cliffs lie to the right as far as (4). The route then veers inland and wends its way through woodland.

TWTSHILL TOWER may have been a look out tower in medieval times; it is certainly ideally placed, overlooking Chepstow and the Severn. Another possibility is that it was a folly built on the whim of some landowner. It now lies within a private garden.

Anticipation at reaching the end of the Offa's Dyke Path grows from now on, where the way leads down to skirt Chepstow and then crosses the A48 and Brunel's railway bridge over the Wye. A short distance beyond here the path reaches the start of the final stretch of the Dyke.

ROUTE DIRECTIONS

1. Turn right and go down to cross a road and on down a surfaced lane between walls. At a T-junction turn left and go up quite steeply. (Chepstow can be reached by continuing ahead at the junction.) At the top of a rise, fork right down a narrower path with views to Chepstow on the right. Emerge at a drive where a right turn leads to the road.
2. Turn right along the road and cross a bridge over the railway and Chepstow bypass. After 80yds, go right into Wyebank Avenue. Go left at the first turn and then, after a few yards, go right down a narrow fenced path. Continue round to the left, with the Wye down to your right, to emerge at a wide grassy verge.
3. Where the verge ends, keep right on a surfaced path between a bungalow on the left and a fence on the right. Bear round left past a sewage works and along a lane with the overgrown Dyke on your left. Continue through a housing estate along Offa's Close and straight ahead along Mercian Way, past an ancient oak with pleasant stone seating and steps. The Dyke on the left is rather well trimmed.
4. Where the road bends right, go left along the bottom end of a grassy area. (The official footpath goes along a fenced-in stretch but this becomes very overgrown.) Turn right down Norse Way and go over wooden sleepers to cross a lane, then continue up a field with the Dyke on your right.
5. On reaching the road cross with care and go up the lane opposite for a few yards. Go right over a stile and follow a path along the top of the Dyke. This final stretch can be very muddy. Go up a final steep section and reach the Offa's Dyke Stone on top of Sedbury Cliff at the end of your journey.

NOTE: It is possible to return to the road by going down right from the Offa's Dyke Stone. This leads to the foreshore and a right of way that leads inland. There is a regular bus service from Beachley to Chepstow.

Chepstow

CHEPSTOW LIES on the western slopes of the River Wye at the river's lowest bridging point. There was an Iron Age hill fort at the Bulwark on the banks of the Wye.

The original castle was built by William Fitz Osborn soon after the Conquest of 1066. His stone keep stood within a walled bailey which ran along the edge of the limestone cliffs above the Wye. Chepstow Castle is the earliest stone defensive work in Britain. It was extended east and west along the ridge over subsequent years until it enclosed the area which has survived today, an elegant and noble ruin.

Chepstow was a walled town. Its historic Port Wall was built during the late 13th century. The wall remains virtually intact and is complemented by the Town Gate at the top of High Street. The town was an important market from Norman times and was also a port and ship-building centre. It declined during the 19th century but is still a busy and thriving shopping centre. The streets and alleyways are pleasingly irregular and mostly sloping, and the descent of Bridge Street from the central Beaufort Square leads past some interesting period houses. Chepstow Museum is in Bridge Street near the castle car park, and repays a visit.

Chepstow has much to offer the walker and casual visitor, not least a visit to the castle. There are a number of first class pubs and restaurants, a range of accommodation including a youth hostel, full shopping facilities and most services. Transport connections can be made via Chepstow station and there are bus services from the town.

Monmouth

MONMOUTH OCCUPIES a strategic position where the Rivers Monnow and Trothy join the Wye. The modern town has been robbed of its river frontage by the A40 but has retained its medieval pattern of streets and lanes. Later Georgian architecture enhanced Monmouth greatly and the modern town has an overall style and atmosphere that is very pleasing. Little outward 'sprawl' into the surrounding low-lying river flats has taken place because of the threat of flooding to new building there. There is little evidence of pre-Roman settlement, but remarkable excavation work by the Monmouth Archaeological Society has uncovered substantial Roman and

Norman remains beneath demolished buildings in Monnow Street, the town's main thoroughfare. Excavations in Monnow Street have drawn thousands of fascinated visitors in recent years.

Saxon settlement at Monmouth was probable, but the town became truly established during the Norman era as an important border fortification. Monmouth Castle, of which little remains, was built in 1071. King Henry V was born in the castle. A Benedictine priory building survives in Priory Street and is now a youth hostel in the tradition of the rather stately hostels of the Wye valley.

On the walker's route into Monmouth lies the town's most striking building, the Monnow Bridge Gatehouse, a 13th century fortification which may also have been used as a market gate and toll gate. Monnow Street retains the irregular line of its original medieval market, widening from Monnow Bridge and then narrowing again where it runs into Agincourt Square.

The Square is hospitably flanked by old coaching inns such as the Kings Head, the Beaufort Arms and the Punch House. A short walk along the pedestrianised Church Street leads to the Church of St Mary with its tall and elegant spire. Apart from the tower, which is 14th century, the church was rebuilt in 1882. It is very wide and high-roofed and has some excellent Victorian stained glass by Charles Kempe.

Monmouth Museum in Priory Street holds a collection of Nelson memorabilia collected originally by Lady Llangattock, the mother of Charles Rolls. Nelson visited Monmouth on two occasions. The naval connection in such a land-locked place is continued on The Kymin with its Naval memorial and its roll call of famous admirals. The town has a good selection of shops including some fascinating antique and fine art shops. There are several inns, restaurants and cafes, and most types of accommodation are available, including camping. Monmouth Leisure Centre, which has a swimming pool and other facilities, is in Old Dixton Road. There are bus connections from Monmouth to other centres.

Left: Chepstow Castle
Below: Monmouth

WYE VALLEY WALK

THE WYE VALLEY WALK is an imaginative modern concept in the best tradition of long-distance walks. The complete route from Chepstow to Rhayader is 110 miles (176km), but the section described here, from Monmouth to Hereford, is just 36 miles (57km). The route is not as demanding as Offa's Dyke but certain stretches can be pretty muddy during wet weather. There are youth hostels at Monmouth and Welsh Bicknor and a few camp sites can be found on or near the path. Hotels and bed-and-breakfast establishments are available at main centres.

The section of the route described in this guide lies within the southern part of the Wye valley, which has been officially designated an Area of Outstanding Natural Beauty. It is not suitable for mountain bikes or horses and it is illegal to cycle where the route follows a public footpath.

This part of the Wye Valley Walk takes a particularly fine route north from Monmouth to pass through the Symonds Yat area and on to Ross-on-Wye. It follows the great lazy curves of the river as far as Kerne Bridge, then veers off through a patchwork of fields and woods. Beyond Ross, the path follows the river once more but again deviates to thread its way through pastoral and apple-orchard country to Mordiford and on to Hereford's cathedral city.

How Caple (top left), a charming hamlet standing high above the river to the north of Ross-on-Wye
The Wye Valley Walk passes close to the summit of Capler Camp (left), near Brockhampton
The Wye makes a huge loop round Huntsham Hill, with Symonds Yat at the neck making a spectacular
viewpoint (above)
Hereford (below) - journey's end

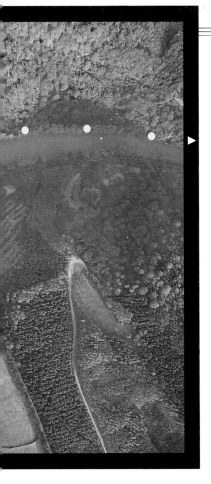

Monmouth to Welsh Bicknor

9¾ miles (15.5km)

This section of the Wye Valley Walk passes through some of the loveliest of the Wye's scenery and includes the popular Symonds Yat. Beyond Symonds Yat there is quieter riverside country. The going is not strenuous although it can be muddy in places during very wet weather.

THIS FIRST STRETCH of the path is a delightful introduction to river walking. From the start at Monmouth the roar of traffic on the accompanying A40 soon fades as the path runs on, fringed with willow, hawthorn, beech and dark-leaved spindle trees all of which hum with insect life in summer and give some wind shelter in winter. To the right the Wye runs dark and deep.

Dixton's Church of St Peter, with its whitewashed plaster walls, is a pleasant diversion. There was a Celtic religious site here called Llandidwg and the west bank of the Wye from Monmouth to just north of Ross lay within the ancient *cymw*, or province, of Erging. This enclave was known also as Archenfield and retained its Celtic identity through a long tradition of Anglo-Welsh harmony during Saxon and Norman times. The Anglicised name of Dixton derives from the old Welsh. The church has traces of herringbone stonework of 1080 but the present structure, with its little broach spire, is 13th century. The interior has seen Victorian restoration. St Peter's escapes too much intrusion from the nearby A40 but the river has made its presence felt dramatically, with spectacular flooding, in the past. Brass markers on the chancel arch record some of the biggest floods, including that of 1947 which reached a height of 6ft 2ins (1.8m).

From St Peter's the path leads on through a kissing-gate and over a footbridge where there is a tang of wild mint in the air. It continues pleasantly along the river bank to reach a rather cramped section. Here the hardcore from the A40 has spilled down the slope and the path can be overgrown in high summer when several shades of red valerian, including white specimens, flourish on the rough slope. The way continues along a pleasant raised section of path, below a walled property, amidst rhododendrons, yew and horse-chestnut.

ROUTE DIRECTIONS

Reach the banks of the Wye by following the directions for Offa's Dyke Path from Monmouth's Agincourt Square (see page 70). Go under the busy A40 via the subway, then turn left along the river bank past the Monmouth Rowing Club and continue along the riverside path to reach the little Church of St Peter at Dixton.

1. Bear left away from the river bank and round a clump of trees, then go right to cross a footbridge over a ditch.
2. Enter woods and go along a muddy and rocky stretch of path where hardcore from the A40 has spilled down the slope. This can be quite awkward and slippery.
3. Cross an open area below a large house with turrets and cupolas and then pass below some greenhouses.

THE WYE IS at its deepest along this section where it runs between the limestone outcrops of Great Doward on the west bank and Lady Park Wood on the east. It is a limestone-rich area which supports many wild plants, including such rarities as the autumn gentian with its purple cylindrical flowers, and the pencilled cranesbill, a garden escapee with pale, purple-veined blooms.

On Great Doward lies King Arthur's Cave but its mythical name belies the cave's antiquity. Excavations, some crudely achieved with explosives in Victorian times, have revealed the bones of mammoth, cave bear, cave lion, bison, woolly rhinoceros and the great Irish deer. Two million years ago, when the sea level was substantially higher, the cave would probably have been on the river's bank. A variety of remains at different levels indicate that the cave was used by various groups through time. Palaeolithic (Stone Age) flints of 30,000 years ago have been found in the lower earth layers and a

nearby rock shelter may have been a Stone Age camp site.

The path along this section runs through areas of coppiced beech and mixed broad-leaved woods. There was much exploitation of this whole area up to last century. Trees, stripped of their bark which was used for tanning, were allowed to die and then cut and floated in rafts downriver to Monmouth sawmills. Much of this still wooded area is now managed and cared for by the Forestry Commission. Walkers should remain aware and careful of the risks of fire.

ROUTE DIRECTIONS

1. Continue into a wooded area, passing a lovely old house on the left.
2. The path winds up left to join a broader track by the ruins of a lime works. Continue past an old iron gate and along a good firm path. The base of the Seven Sisters Rocks shows through the trees on the left. A steeply rising path leads uphill from the main path at one point. This leads to the base of Seven Sisters Rocks then veers left and steeply upwards to the summit of Great Doward.
3. Reach an open grassy meadow at The Biblins. The Forestry Commission has a camping site here for organised parties only. Cross The Biblins bridge. Only six people at a time should cross the bridge, and jogging is not advised!
4. Turn left along a surfaced track. At a staggered junction, keep left on to a riverside track which soon narrows and becomes overgrown. The path runs parallel to a forestry road all the way to Symonds Yat East.
5. Where the path rises to meet the forestry road, bear down and go over a stile into an open meadow. Turn right along the riverbank to Symonds Yat East.

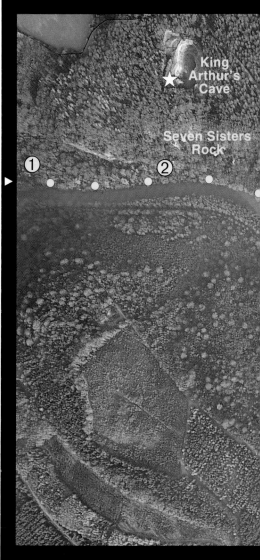

The Biblins

③

④

⑤

Lady Park Wood

ROUTE DIRECTIONS

1. Just past Saracens Head and the Wyedene Canoe and Adventure Centre, bear left off the road and go through the entrance to a caravan site car park. Do not continue into the caravan park. Instead cross the car park diagonally left and continue right along a narrow path between the river bank and the fenced edge of the caravan park. Continue along a field edge.

2. At the ferry point opposite Ye Olde Ferrie Inn, go right to the road. Cross the road and bear left into trees. Reach another road and turn left for 100yds then go right into the trees to join a forestry road.

3. Where the road levels off and curves gently round to the right, go left and down some steep wooden steps. There are open views across the river to Goodrich with its church and steeple. Continue steeply down to where the path levels off, then continue through a shaded area

passing old ruined buildings and large boulders of quartz conglomorate.

4. Go down wooden steps to the river bank by some huge boulders. Pass a charming little house and soon follow the path into an open area from where it winds uphill and away from the river. Cross a forestry road and continue up steep steps opposite.

5. Reach a T-junction. (Yat Rock can be reached in about 15 minutes by going right and steeply uphill to a road where a left turn leads to access to the viewpoint area.) For the main route go left, descending gently to reach a very rocky section of path above a house overlooking the river.

6. Turn right along the broad track of a dismantled railway line. Note the old rail sleepers at the side of the track.

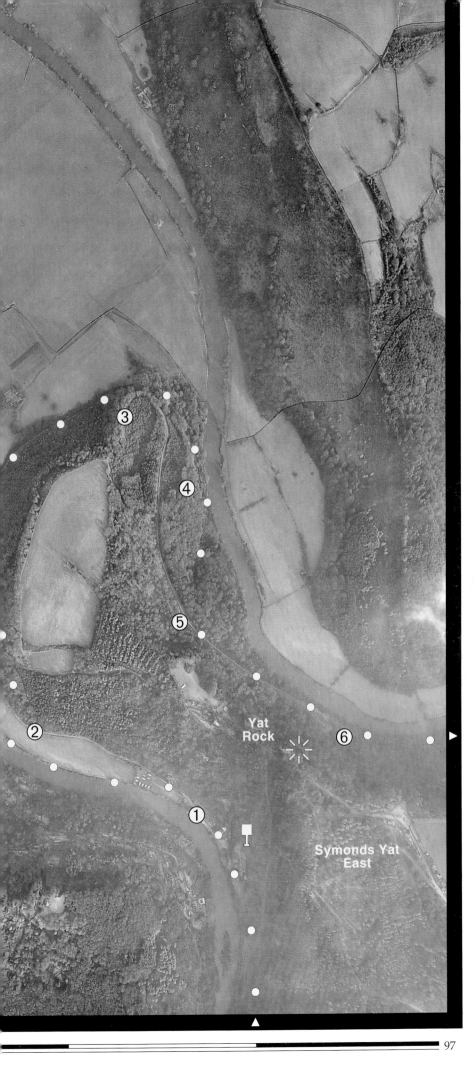

Yat
Rock

③

④

⑤

②

⑥

①

Symonds Yat
East

ROUTE DIRECTIONS

Sheep are likely to be grazing in the open pasture along this section. Dogs should be kept under strict control.

1. Continue along the pleasant track through open pasture.
2. Go over a stile and through some woods, then go down some wooden steps on the left and over a stile to continue by the river through grassy fields

YAT ROCK CAN BE gained directly from Symonds Yat East by following a path starting between the Royal Hotel and the garden of the Forest View Hotel. Symonds Yat East has several hotels, restaurants, cafés, inns and gift shops. Enjoyable river trips can be taken from here and there are hand-operated chain ferries to Symonds Yat West where there are attractions such as the Jubilee Park, the Tropical Bird Park, World of Butterflies and the Museum of Mazes within easy reach. Symonds Yat West also has a large number of hotels and guesthouses.

Yat Rock and Coldwell Rocks lie on the flanks of Huntsham Hill within a shapely loop of the River Wye. The lofty height of Huntsham's limestone mass has meant that the river has been unable to breach the narrow neck of the meander to leave a classic ox-bow lake. Instead, the high ground of Yat Rock separates the river to east and west by a mere ¼ mile (400m). The cliffs of Yat Rock and Coldwell Rocks rise to a height of 400ft (121m) and are most impressive on the east side of Yat Rock where the vertical theme is extended south to Coldwell Rocks. Symonds Yat takes the first part of its name from a 17th century High Sheriff of Herefordshire, Robert Symonds. A 'yat' is a local name for gate or passageway through steep heights.

The top of Yat Rock has a cabin shop where refreshments are available. There are also viewing platforms, from which there are wide-ranging views of the Wye and its wooded gorge, and across all the old counties of the border region. From these platforms RSPB wardens are often on duty with information about Yat Rock's famous peregrine falcons, which have successfully nested annually on the cliffs since 1982. Peregrines were previously brought close to extinction by culling and through absorbing pesticides in the food chain.

The section of path which winds round the base of Huntsham Hill from Symonds Yat East passes through quiet and lovely river-bank countryside. The woods are a mix of broad-leaved trees and conifers, including oak and ash, beech, lime, sweet-chestnut, birch, larch and yew. Douglas fir and European larch are a special feature in the woods of Yat Rock. The earliest flowers seen alongside the path are primroses and celandine. In February snowdrops brighten the dark rocky ground of Elliot's Wood on the east side of Huntsham Hill.

The Museum of Mazes, one of the attractions in the area

Coldwell
Rocks

Welsh Bicknor to Ross-on-Wye

7½ miles (12km)

The way to Ross lies along the river bank from Welsh Bicknor to Kerne Bridge where the path then leaves the river and heads inland through a pleasing mix of farmland and wooded hills. There are some steep sections but the going is generally easy. Paths can become quite muddy during prolonged wet weather.

ROUTE DIRECTIONS

1. Pass a substantial factory on the right. Go over a stile and continue along a grassy track to pass a water bailiff's hut with a fish windvane.

2. Pass under the disused railway bridge and go up steps on the right alongside the factory. Cross the railway bridge and turn right alongside the river.

3. Pass a house on the left and bear up slightly left along a track, which leads past the handsome youth hostel at Welsh Bicknor. Continue along the track in front of the hostel to pass St Margaret's Church. Follow the the river as it curves north, opposite Lydbrook, and enter Thomas Wood.

Thomas Wood

Looking back towards Welsh Bicknor before entering Thomas Wood

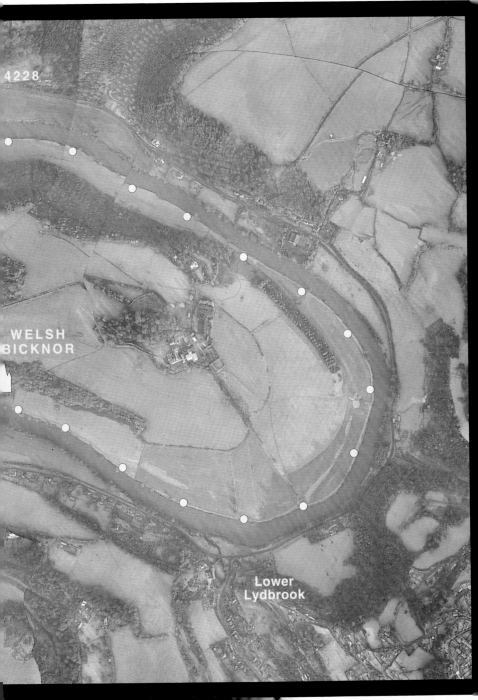

4228

WELSH
BICKNOR

Lower
Lydbrook

ROUTE DIRECTIONS

1. Continue along the river bank and go over a stile into a wooded area. The path here may become unpleasantly overgrown with Himalayan balsam during the summer months. Pass a small cottage on the left. Go down some steep wooden steps and continue to the road at the five-arched Kerne Bridge.

2. Turn right over Kerne Bridge, then go immediately right along a path to reach the Kerne Bridge picnic site. Cross the B4234, with care, enter a side road, then turn left up a lane. At the top of the slope, go right up some steps and on to a path. Climb more steps then go right up a drive. Cross a drive and continue on a rising path amidst trees.

3. Reach a T-junction with a farm track. Turn left and pass Oak Gables, then turn off left down a path that leads behind a house. Continue down through woods and past a small quarry on your right. At a Y-junction, keep left down a concreted track past Cherry Tree Cottage. The River Wye can be glimpsed through the trees just beyond here.

4. Just before the track reaches the B4234 turn right up a surfaced drive. (There is a fine view of Goodrich Castle from the main road.)

Where the drive curves round to the right, continue straight on along a broad earthy track which soon turns into a tree-lined path. Cross a concrete drive by a building and pick up a narrow path opposite.

5. Come out on a road by a house. Cross the road, bearing down left, then turn up right by a public footpath signpost and follow a gravelled drive towards Bucks Mill Cottage. Bear round left to pass the side door of the cottage and go down some very steep steps to a stile into a field. Bear downhill to the left to cross a stream, then continue uphill to go over a stile into trees. Go left over another stile and along a shady track.

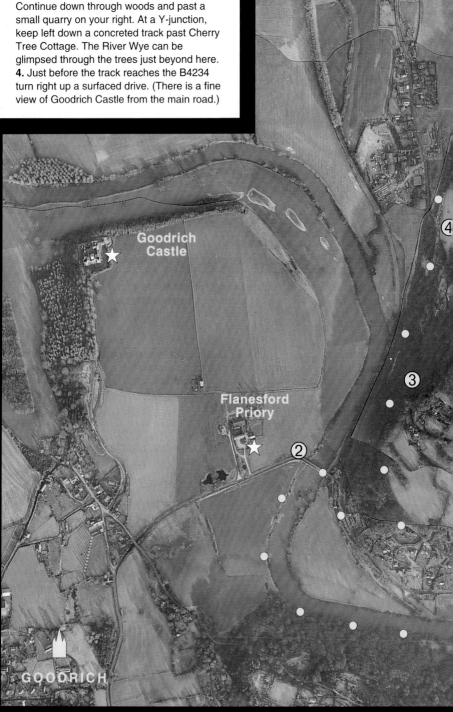

Goodrich Castle

Flanesford Priory

GOODRICH

⑤

THE DOMINANT FEATURE of the area is well preserved Goodrich Castle which lies on the western bank of the Wye. Its resilient red sandstone walls, with the contrasting green-hued stonework of the Norman keep, stand out dramatically on its grassy bluff. The castle has survived remarkably well in spite of bombardment during the civil war of the 17th century when it was laid siege to by Parliamentarian forces using a huge mortar called 'Roaring Meg'. The castle has an intriguing complex of passageways and rooms, including a chapel and dungeon. In the care of English Heritage, it is open daily throughout the year except for Monday closures from October to April.

The Church of St Giles at Goodrich village has a fine tall spire and an attractive Victorian sundial on its wall. There is a post office and inn at Goodrich. Just to the west of Kerne Bridge are the remains of 14th century Flanesford Priory.

Goodrich Castle, now in the care of English Heritage

Fort

Chase
Wood

③

②

①

Walford church at the tiny hamlet across the river from Goodrich Castle
Below: Chase Wood Hill with Ross-on-Wye beyond

THIS SECTION OF the route runs along quiet lanes and through small areas of woodland. It rises steeply at (3), over the impressive hill of Chase Wood with its mix of broad-leaved trees and conifers. The summit of Chase Wood Hill was the site of a substantial hill fort of the Iron Age established about the 4th century BC. Flint blades have been found on Chase Wood Hill, indicating much earlier activity by Stone Age man.

The countryside north of Symonds Yat becomes increasingly pastoral across the rich farmlands of the Herefordshire Plain. Herefordshire is famous for its cattle. The breed developed from plough oxen and was improved by the Tomkins family during the late 18th century. The pure Hereford, with its fine 'marbled' beef and its rich milk, is said to have been bred from a famous cow called Silver, left to Benjamin Tomkins by his father Richard. Original colours were black and white, but a red and white strain proved to be dominant. By the time of Benjamin Tomkins's death in 1815 Herefords were being exported to North America and by the end of the 19th century the breed was established in Argentina where it numbered millions of head.

ROUTE DIRECTIONS

1. Cross a road and follow a broad stony track as it contours round a hillside. Where the track becomes surfaced at a T-junction, turn left down a rough track past Still Meadow Cottage. At Rose Cottage turn left off the track, go over a stile and cross a small field into trees, then turn right.

2. Cross three stiles in quick succession, crossing the track to Craig Farm on the way. Go down the side of a field and reach a road. Turn left for 100yds, then turn right up through three farm gates to continue direct along a path through fields.

3. Climb very steeply up through the trees of Chase Wood. At the top of the steepest rise there is a T-junction. Turn right, bear left at the next junction, then bear left on to a broad forestry track. Follow the good wide track steadily downhill.

ROUTE DIRECTIONS

1. Reach a crossing of tracks just beyond a wooden barrier. Go straight across and continue down an earthy track just left of the buildings of Hill Farm. The path leads through Merrivale Wood, a designated national reserve which is in the care of the Herefordshire Nature Trust. Go over a stile into a field, left for a short distance, then left again at an oak tree. Continue down a broad, earthy ride, bearing round to the right. Go over two stiles in quick succession and continue steeply left, down a field.

2. At the field bottom turn left through a kissing-gate and follow a path down through trees to emerge on to a surfaced road at Acton Court Adventure Centre. Continue down Penyard Lane, past a small industrial estate on the right. At a T-junction, turn left and continue along Alton Street, passing a hospital on the right and Deanhill Park on the left.

3. Turn left at a busy crossroads. Note Toll Cottage opposite. (Ross town centre can be reached by turning right.) Continue past St Frances of Rome Catholic Church. At Kent Avenue, cross the busy road, with care. The Prince of Wales pub is on the opposite corner. Go down Ashfield Park Road and continue along a fenced road with Ashfield Park School on your left.

4. Bear round left through a kissing-gate and along a path skirting the school playing field. Go down stone steps, then turn right on to a track, then quickly left bearing right down wooden steps and into a car park.

5. Continue along a surfaced path and go through a tunnel under a bridge. Before reaching public toilets, bear left across the grass and cross a road to the riverside. Go right along the riverbank.

6. At the end of a playing field, cross the track to the clubhouse of a rowing club. Go over a foot bridge and through a kissing-gate, then continue left around the edge of a field. Go through another kissing-gate and across a footbridge to regain the riverbank. Go right under Bridstow Bridge with the A40 above, and continue along the left edge of two fields.

Ross-on-Wye to Capler Camp

9¼ miles (14.8km)

The Wye Valley Walk leads north from Ross along the banks of the river for some distance. It then cuts across one of the Wye's emphatic meanders at King's Caple. The going is not strenuous and the countryside is pleasantly varied.

Monks
Grove
Wood

ROSS-ON-WYE, the main town of south Herefordshire, lies below Chase Wood Hill. It rises in terraces above a horseshoe-shaped meander of the Wye and is crowned by the Church of St Mary the Virgin standing on a sandstone bluff. Modern Ross is hedged in by major roads to the north and west but the town rises above all that and retains its persuasive charm. At the heart of the town is the 17th century Market House, a striking building of red sandstone with an upper storey resting on pillars and archways. The main streets of the town radiate from here.

Opposite the Market House stands the 17th century half-timbered house of John Kyrle, a local philanthropist. Kyrle was immortalised as the 'Man of Ross' in the Moral Essays of Alexander Pope who may, or may not, have been satirising Kyrle's apparently compulsive generosity. Kyrle not only gave money and goods to the local poor but he greatly improved Ross through his instinct for thoughtful town planning. He laid out the attractive Prospect Gardens alongside the parish church. Ross's first water supply was financed by Kyrle, who also planted many trees and set up public seats throughout the town.

Kyrle financed an extension of the church tower by an additional 47ft (14m), a gesture which says something about his sense of place. He was certainly a gregarious man who craved company and believed in the community. His philanthropy included practical gestures such as baking bread every Saturday morning and then distributing the loaves to the poor. Kyrle sent food each day to the local almshouses, paid for the education of some local children and apprentices, and dispensed herbal medicines. As a footnote to all this philanthropy was that, 50 years after his death, many of Kyrle's structural innovations had been neglected or even vandalised. Later generations have recognised the Man of Ross for his superlative goodness.

Modern Ross would certainly have impressed Kyrle. It is an attractive and well-kept town which bustles with life and has a number of good inns, including the inevitable Man of Ross in Wye Street. There are also restaurants, cafés and a whole range of accommodation, numerous shops and other facilities. There is a tourist information centre in Broad Street, the street that runs downhill from the Market House.

ROUTE DIRECTIONS

. Where the river bends sharply west, continue north for a short distance, alongside a drainage channel.

. Turn left on to the track of a dismantled railway line. After 100yds, go right off the track and down steps and over a stile into a field. Keep forward with a fence on your right.

. Reach the banks of the river once more.

Go through a metal gate and continue forward on a rough track for 50yds, then go left through a gate into a field. Walk forward with a hedge on your left, and, where the hedge ends, go forward to another hedge and keep this on your right. In the corner of the field, go over a stile into Monks Grove Wood.

The Church of St Mary in Ross

THE RIVER WYE along this section of the path has some excellent fishing. Anyone wishing to fish the Wye must first acquire the necessary licence from the National Rivers Authority and must also obtain permission to fish particular areas from the owner or controlling authority.

The Wye has long been famous as a fishing river. There are 29 species of fish ranging from minnows and sticklebacks, chubb, roach and pike, to trout and the mighty salmon. Commercial salmon fishing on the Wye has had a colourful and often destructive history. The river environment has remained healthy for fish because medieval and Victorian industry did not develop into the intensive manufacturing of modern times. Industrial pollution is minimal, agricultural practices have seen a steady decline in use of potentially damaging chemicals, and generous rainfall ensures that fast-moving tributaries feed clean water into the main river.

Exploitation by man has been the most damaging influence because of sporadic and heavy netting for salmon over the centuries. Fishing rights were once owned by the monasteries but fell to the crown after the Dissolution. The building of numerous weirs caused problems for the salmon in their migration upstream to their spawning grounds. A 17th century writer spoke of the Wye at Chepstow being 'swollen with a sea of salmon'.

Uncontrolled catching of salmon by net, spear and rod continued until the latter part of last century when thoughtful conservation and practical control became established. Today, fishing on the Wye is strictly controlled. There is an average rod catch of 4,000 salmon some of which reach 40lbs in weight.

The life cycle of the salmon involves a remarkable migratory cycle. Spawning takes place on clean gravel beds in shallow but fast-flowing water at the headwaters of rivers. Eggs are laid in small trenches which the female salmon excavates with sweeps of her tail. The eggs are then fertilised by 'milt' secreted by the male salmon. The hatched fish, called fry, remain in the headwaters of the river for several years, growing into parr and then smolt, at which time they begin their migration to the sea and on to Arctic waters.

Growth at sea is rapid due to rich feeding on shrimps and prawns. Within a year or two the salmon begins its unerring journey back to its birthplace there to begin the breeding cycle once more during November and December. The salmon's strength and drive are legendary. It travels upstream, surmounting powerful rapids and waterfalls, and can clear a 10ft (3m) fall with one leap. Higher obstacles are often 'climbed' by the salmon leaping from ledge to ledge using the immense power of its tail and even by harnessing the power from the water's downward thrust.

Arable land occupies the flood plain of the Wye as it meanders north of Ross

ROUTE DIRECTIONS

1. Leave Monks Grove by a stile into a field. At the end of the field go through a gate and along the edge of the next field. Foy church can be seen on the opposite bank of the river.
2. Just before the track reaches the end of the field, bear right off the track and through a metal gate to the right of a mature oak. Continue on an enclosed path with a plantation of conifers on your right. Continue beyond the plantation with a hedge on your left to reach a road opposite Orchard Cottage.
3. Turn left down the road past past Foy suspension bridge. Pass the Court Farm Activity Centre and reach Hole-in-the-Wall.

Foy Bridge

HOLE-IN-THE-WALL

HOLE-IN-THE-WALL is believed to have gained its name from a Victorian drinking house that flourished here. The road walking along this section is undemanding but hardly inspiring. Tall ash trees line the way on the landward side with beech trees alongside the river. The openness of this riverside landscape contrasts with the Lower Wye where limestone cliffs contain the river on a relatively direct course. Here the flat alluvial plains encourage extraordinary meanders. West of How Caple the river swings in a great curve past Sellack to Hoarwithy and then back east past Ballingham.

Within the bend of the river lies the village of King's Caple. All of these villages have distinctive churches with St Catherine's at Hoarwithy being of particular interest. It is a Victorian building of an imaginative design which was none too common at a time when so many churches were blandly restored. The church is in the Italianate style with external cloisters and a square tower with pyramid roof. The interior has Byzantine and Romanesque features.

How Caple also has an impressive church, which was rebuilt in the late 17th century. The miraculous powers of St Thomas of Hereford are linked with an incident at How Caple in medieval times. Hereford Cathedral records show that a local boy fell in to the river at How Caple and was thought to be dead when his body was recovered. But his family made a candle as an offering to St Thomas and within hours the boy recovered. Modern medicine might find a different explanation for the phenomenon.

ROUTE DIRECTIONS

1. Continue from Hole-in-the-Wall along a metalled road through Perrystone Estate.
2. Where the road crosses a cattle grid, turn off left immediately before a white gate. Go down open ground to the river's edge, then go right over a stile and a plank bridge into a field. Continue through fields with a hedge to your left. Pass How Caple on your right, then turn left along a road for 150yds.
3. Just after a telephone box, turn right on to a drive. Continue past a house on the right and go forward into a field, keeping ahead with a hedge on your left.

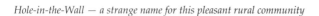

Hole-in-the-Wall — a strange name for this pleasant rural community

Capler
Camp

④

③

②

TOTNER

①

ON THIS SECTION, pleasant walking leads away from the river and up to the impressive site of the Iron Age Capler Camp. From the crossroads just south of Capler Lodge a road runs east to the thatched Church of All Saints at Brockhampton. There was a medieval church at nearby Brockhampton Court but in 1901 the architect William Lethaby built All Saints, incorporating elements of the Arts and Crafts movement in happy conjunction with an overall medieval style. All Saints is a truly delightful building with its thatched roof, timbered belfry and decorated tower. Inside the church, concrete arches and vaulting, beautifully carved oak furnishings and exquisite stained glass continue the stylish theme. An anonymous donor has embellished the church further with embroidered images of wild flowers on the altar cloth and hymn book covers.

ROUTE DIRECTIONS

1. Go right over a wooden footbridge and then straight across a field to a gap and enclosed path which leads to the road at Totner. Turn left and go steeply uphill for ⅓ mile (500m).
2. Turn left down a farm track. Bear right at a corner by an oak tree to reach a road by some houses. Turn right, then immediately bear left down a broad track to reach a road.

3 Turn left at the road. Do not take the signposted track that leads off to the right. Instead, continue along the road past the attractive picnic area of Capler Viewpoint. Pass Capler Lodge, then go right along a track into fine mature woodland. Walkers are asked not to enter the adjoining woods which are private property.
4. Reach a T-junction and turn right. When the track bears up left, continue straight ahead along a short section of path and over a stile into open ground. Follow the bank of Capler Camp to some buildings.

BROCKHAMPTON

N

Capler Camp to Hereford

9¼ miles (14.8km)

The main part of the route to Mordiford passes through typical Herefordshire countryside of rich pastures, apple orchards, and small farms within a network of narrow lanes. It then leads alongside the River Lugg and through the outskirts of Hereford.

ROUTE DIRECTIONS

1. Continue past the buildings where Capler Camp ends. Follow the track where it bears round right, then go left off the track by an old apple tree. Go down to a stile and then steeply down steps and a path into the valley bottom. Continue in the same direction, passing a house and barn on the left to reach a stile.

2 Go immediately left to a stile into a farm road. Turn right, then turn left at another road and after 60 yds turn right on to a farm track. Soon, at a gateway, turn right off the track and go down the field edge to cross a stile in the bottom hedge.

3. Go immediately right to follow the edge of the field and go through a gate in its bottom edge. Continue up a slope, ignoring a waymarked stile on the left. Instead, follow the field edge uphill to another stile, then bear left over stiles with fine views to the left. Pass a small empty building on the right and continue along the left edge of a meadow.

4. Go over a stile into the nature reserve of Paget's Wood and Lea Wood. At a junction of paths, keep left then go down the right-hand branch marked as a bridlepath. Continue along this path to a gate and stile and cross an open meadow with a road down to the left. Continue with a fence on the right to reach a road.

5. Cross the road and go along a surfaced track to the right of Common Hill Farm, then bear up left on to a shady track. Bear sharp right by a covered reservoir. Continue through woodland along a raised bank and past a welcome wooden bench, courtesy of the Herefordshire Nature Trust. There are fine views from here.

6. Go down some steps and pass through a flower-filled clearing with beech trees and dog rose. Reach an open, surfaced area by scattered houses. Ignore turnings to the left and keep ahead up a gravelly track opposite.

7. Continue along the track with open views to the right. Just past a house on the left the track becomes a delightful tree-lined path. Fownhope, with its striking church, can be seen down to the left. Keep high and right at a junction and soon pass a little house nestling amidst the trees down to your left.

Capler Camp, south of Fownhope

ROUTE DIRECTIONS

1. Reach a road and cross it diagonally right to go through a gate. Bear round right, then go up left through a gate and continue up a rough track. Keep ahead across an open field where the track fades, to reach a stile by a gate in the middle of the far hedge.

2. Go through a gate and keep straight ahead with a hedge on your right. Where the fence bends sharply right, keep straight ahead to pass a solitary oak.

3. Go through a gate and along a rough farm track. Continue through a farmyard, then turn sharp left along a roughly surfaced road. Just past a house with double garages bear right by Woodlands Cottage and go down a grassy path and over a stile.

4. Continue down through orchards to reach a stile just beyond a willow tree.

THE PATH THROUGH the latter part of this section leads down through orchards towards Mordiford. These orchards are symbolic of Hereford's great tradition of cider making. The industry goes back to medieval times and, in Herefordshire, cider making from apples and perry from pears is integral to the life of the county. Cider has even influenced the great religious traditions. In Hereford Cathedral's famous chained library is a 'cider bible' of the 14th century in which the phrase 'strong drink' has been frequently translated throughout into the vernacular 'cider'.

Praised as the 'white wine of England', cider has been produced in the county from a host of colourfully named fruit, the taste and texture of which few modern palates have appreciated. At one time there were over 360 different varieties of apple. Many have been lost, but up to 100 varieties are still grown in specialist orchards.

Cider became less popular as a staple drink nationally after the end of the Napoleonic Wars when cheap wine from France became readily available. But in 1888, Percy Bulmer of Credenhill, to the west of Hereford, began commercial production. Bulmer was the son of a local vicar. He set up in business in Hereford in 1888 and produced 4,000 gallons in his first season. Today, 50,000 tons of apples are likely to be pressed each season at Bulmer's modern plant where steel tanks hold 1.6 million gallons each and an average of 15 million gallons is stored.

Fownhope, a prosperous village close to the Wye

THE APPLE BLOSSOM path to Mordiford takes the walker into the heart of the village and within easy reach of refreshments. Mordiford is an attractive village with a fine terrace of old cottages running along the curve of the main street. The bridge is extremely old, with a surviving 14th century span and 16th century stonework. Just south of the bridge the River Lugg enters the Wye at the optimum of a sharp bend. This leads to flooding of the surrounding area at times and embankments have been raised for some distance to alleviate the problem.

Mordiford Bridge and village have suffered some spectacular floods. In 1811 the river expanded to a width of nearly 200ft (60m) and a 20ft (6m) wall of floodwater was reported as destroying buildings and drowning several people. Bridge and village have survived intact.

Mordiford church has not survived Victorian meddling, however. The original central tower was demolished in the early part of last century and the present rather stolid tower was built as a replacement. An old motif of a green dragon once graced the old tower. This mythical beast was said to have terrorised the neighbourhood until shot by a condemned prisoner who volunteered his services in hope of a pardon. He hid in an empty cider barrel, probably having drunk the contents first, and fired an arrow through the bunghole. With its dying breath, the dragon rather thoughtlessly incinerated the barrel and its occupant. There be no dragons in Mordiford today, but there are pubs, and a post office and village shop.

The path leads on from Mordiford along an embankment flanking the River Lugg. It passes just north of Hampton

Bishop where the Norman church has three reredoses, one in use and the others as interesting relics. A reredos is the decorated screen normally found behind the altar and below the east window of churches.

To the south-west of Hampton Bishop, across the main road and the River Wye,

Mordiford, where the Wye and the Lugg meet, is prone to flooding

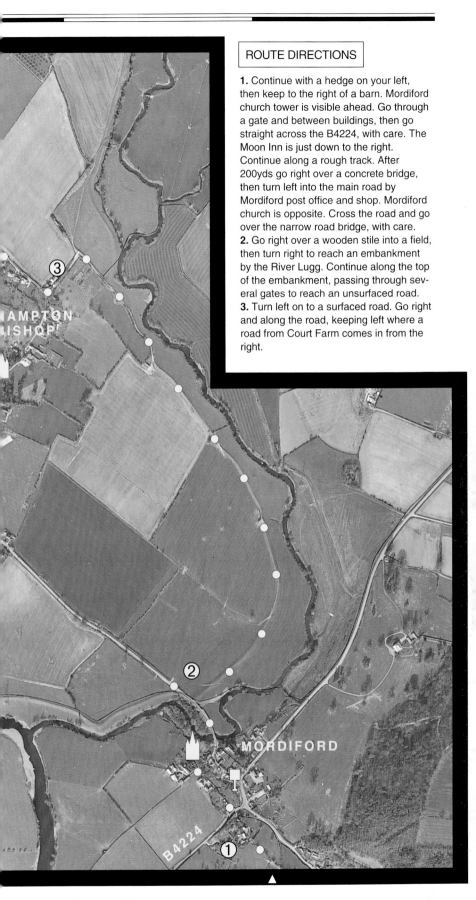

1. Continue with a hedge on your left, then keep to the right of a barn. Mordiford church tower is visible ahead. Go through a gate and between buildings, then go straight across the B4224, with care. The Moon Inn is just down to the right. Continue along a rough track. After 200yds go right over a concrete bridge, then turn left into the main road by Mordiford post office and shop. Mordiford church is opposite. Cross the road and go over the narrow road bridge, with care.
2. Go right over a wooden stile into a field, then turn right to reach an embankment by the River Lugg. Continue along the top of the embankment, passing through several gates to reach an unsurfaced road.
3. Turn left on to a surfaced road. Go right and along the road, keeping left where a road from Court Farm comes in from the right.

is the ridge of Dinedor Hill on whose southern bluff lies the site of a substantial Iron Age camp. Roman remains such as pottery sherds may indicate that Dinedor was occupied by local people for far longer than most of the hillcamps, such as nearby Capler.

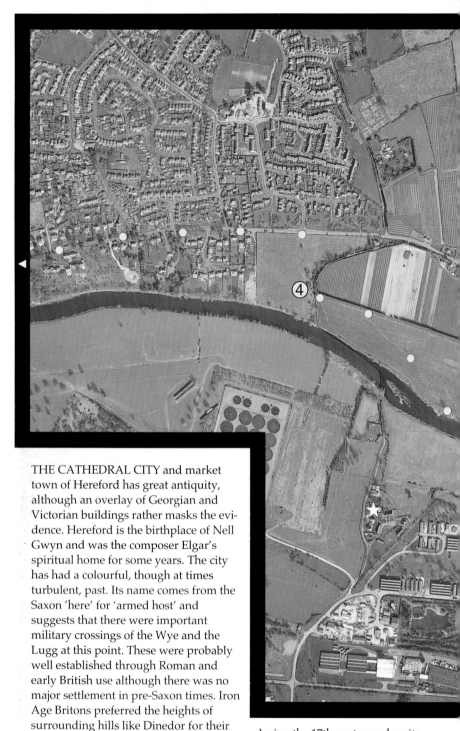

THE CATHEDRAL CITY and market town of Hereford has great antiquity, although an overlay of Georgian and Victorian buildings rather masks the evidence. Hereford is the birthplace of Nell Gwyn and was the composer Elgar's spiritual home for some years. The city has had a colourful, though at times turbulent, past. Its name comes from the Saxon 'here' for 'armed host' and suggests that there were important military crossings of the Wye and the Lugg at this point. These were probably well established through Roman and early British use although there was no major settlement in pre-Saxon times. Iron Age Britons preferred the heights of surrounding hills like Dinedor for their settlements.

Hereford developed on a level site between the Rivers Wye and Lugg and became established as a Saxon community in the 7th century, during which time the cathedral was founded. By the 11th century the basis of the present cathedral was established and Hereford expanded throughout the Norman era.

By the late 13th century the city fathers felt confident and arrogant enough to state that Hereford was 'the principle city of all the market towns between the Severn and the sea'. The city experienced siege and battle, not least during the 17th century when its reputation as a Royalist and Catholic stronghold drew down the wrath of Parliamentary forces and led to final capture in 1645.

Hereford is a delightful riverside city with many attractive walks along the banks of the Wye and through attractive park land. The city's crowning glory is its cathedral, a compelling and solidly reassuring building which may not have the elegance and grace of mightier structures but has the awesome dignity which only Romanesque architecture of the Norman period can give. Among the cathedral's many glories is the 13th

ROUTE DIRECTIONS

. Just beyond a bend in the road turn off
ght and go along a path between two
ouses. Continue through a field, keeping a
ence to your left, and carry straight on when
he fence bends away left. Reach the main
4224 by a telephone box. Go right for 50yds,
hen cross the busy road, with care, opposite
he entrance to Haven and White Haven.

. Go left through a wooden gate then up
ome steps and over a stile on to an embankment. Continue to another stile, then go
mmediately left and over a footbridge. Reach
he River Wye and continue ahead along the
iver bank.

3. At the end of a fourth long field, bear up to
the right towards the right corner of a field by
a line of conifers.

4. Go over a stile and then go right up a well-
worn path to reach the main road opposite
Sudbury Avenue. Turn left and continue for
about a mile (1.6km) through a built-up area.

century Mappa Mundi, an early map of
the world, drawn on vellum. The
cathedral also harbours a wonderful
chained library of about 1,500 rare books,
mainly of theology, history and music,
that reflects Hereford's reputation as a
centre of intellectual brilliance during the
12th century.

Other fine buildings include the 17th
century Old House in High Town and
the nearby 13th century Booth House,
which is now an hotel. The City Museum
and Art gallery is in Broad Street and the
St John and Coningsby Medieval
Museum is in Widemarsh Street with the
Blackfriars Gardens next door. The town
hall is in St Owen Street where there is

an adjoining tourist information centre.

Hereford's famous cattle market
between Edgar Street and New Market
Street is entertaining, especially on a
busy Wednesday morning. There is a
Cider Museum in Pomona Place off
Whitecross Road and Bulmers Cider Mill
is in Plough Lane, which is also off
Whitecross Road.

The town is extremely well supplied
with all types of accommodation and
has many services and facilities. There is
a sports and leisure centre in Holme
Road and a leisure pool off St Martin's
Street. Bus and rail connections can be
made from the city to all parts of the
country.

ROUTE DIRECTIONS

1. Go under a railway bridge and then turn left up Park Street. At the far end of Park Street, turn right into Green Street, then go first left down Vicarage Road with the Church of St James on your right. On your left there is a row of interesting alms houses.

2. Pass St James Primary School and go forward through a metal kissing-gate and on down a surfaced path to the river, from where a right turn leads to Victoria Bridge. The centre of Hereford can be reached from here. Alternatively, a pleasant walk along the south bank of the Wye leads to Wye Bridge from where the cathedral and the city centre is quickly reached.

Right inset: Hereford Cathedral

Index to both routes

Garth Hill towards Knighton

Coppet Hill and River Wye near Goodrich

Intriguingly named Bagpiper's Tump, a feature south of Mordiford

Useful Addresses

The following bodies may be contacted at the addresses given for any further information required.

CADW (Welsh Historic Monuments)
Brunel House
2 Fitzalan Road
Cardiff
South Glamorgan CF2 1UY

Countryside Commission
John Dower House
Crescent Place
Cheltenham
Glos GL50 3RA

Countryside Council for Wales
Ladywell House
Newtown
Powys SY16 1RD

English Heritage
Northminster House
Peterborough
Cambs PE1 1UA

Offa's Dyke Association
West Street
Knighton
Powys LD7 1EW

Ramblers' Association
1/5 Wandsworth Road
London SW8 2LJ

Youth Hostels Association
Trevelyan House
8 St Stephens Hill
St Albans
Herts AL1 2DY

Wales Tourist Board
see CADW

The publishers would like to thank the county councils of Powys, Gwent, Hereford and Worcester and Gloucestershire; the Wardens and Rangers of the Wye Valley Countryside Service; the Countryside Commission; the Countryside Council for Wales; CADW; English Heritage; the Offas's Dyke Association and the Kington History Society for their help in the preparation of this book.